Praise for *Leaflets of* ı

"*Leaflets of the Russian Revolution* offers a street-level view of the unfolding of the Russian Revolution in 1917, especially in Petrograd. These well-translated leaflets are a rich source for understanding how activists brought to life seemingly abstract ideas like democracy, freedom, socialism, power, and revolution itself. The language of these texts is full of emotion, experience, and determination to change the world. The book also contains documents about the mobilization of Red Guards, trade unions, and other organizations. Barbara Allen's introduction, annotations, and conclusion put this all in clear and essential context."
—**Mark Steinberg**, author of *The Russian Revolution, 1905–1921*

"Authentic human voices are what we hear in these leaflets from the Russian Revolution of 1917. The leaflets, emanating from different socialist parties and workers' organizations, re-create all the vividness and excitement of contemporary debates, while the helpful introduction and notes provide the necessary historical context." —**Sheila Fitzpatrick**, University of Sydney

"This fascinating collection of leaflets from revolutionary 1917 permits readers to experience the immediacy and passion of revolutionary actors. As a collection of primary documents from a critical moment in world history, it is sure to be a valuable teaching resource."
—**Diane P. Koenker**, UCL School of Slavonic and East European Studies

"In this valuable volume, Barbara Allen furnishes all those interested in the Russian Revolution with an important collection of political leaflets reflecting the epoch-defining struggle for power in 1917 Russia. Allen's fine translations and insightful introductions add to the value of the collection."
—**Alexander Rabinowitch**, author of *The Bolsheviks in Power*

"An indispensable collection. These texts, and Barbara Allen's expert curation and explication, bring to vivid life the astonishing tussles, turns, and transformations of 1917, Russia's revolutionary year." —**China Miéville**

"The leaflets, nicely translated, take the reader into the fervent debates between Bolsheviks and Mensheviks during the 1917 Revolution. Allen pays particular attention to Alexander Shlyapnikov, a level-headed Bolshevik metal worker who was involved in party and union organizing. She also provides clear, comprehensive introductions to the materials. The result is a collection that goes beyond the party luminaries and into the ranks of lower-ranking activists. Most of these materials heretofore have been available only in Russian." —Barbara Clements

"Leaflets were an important means of communication and propaganda in the Russian Revolution. This richly annotated and expertly translated selection offers a vital and fascinating insight into a range of left outlooks as Bolsheviks, Mensheviks, SRs, and Interdistricters grappled with the major issues of the day, including the war and a deepening economic collapse. It crucially forefronts the aspirations of trades unions and workers, and illustrates how their hopes and dreams were lost in the Revolution's survival. This primary source reader is essential reading for all students of the world historical event that was the Russian Revolution."

—Ian D. Thatcher, professor of history, Ulster University, UK

"A fine collection of important leaflets from 1917 that present many of the key issues of the day, especially as they affected—and reflected—workers' lives. It outlines the range of views and their evolution. It also focuses on the important, but often forgotten, Bolshevik leader Alexander Shlyapnikov."

—Rex A. Wade

"Barbara Allen has produced a collection of sources that take us right to the heart of the great Russian political debate of 1917. The lifeblood of this debate was the political pamphlet, produced locally and addressing issues at short notice. They were the predecessors of today's blogs and tweets. This fine selection gives us a penetrating insight into the fundamental fabric of the political and social revolution."

—Christopher Read, professor of modern European history, University of Warwick, UK

"Concerns of the streets and shop floors ring out in Barbara Allen's illuminating collection of leaflets and appeals from 1917, Russia's year of revolution. Newly available source material, chosen or written by Alexander Shlyapnikov, metalworker and first Soviet commissar of labor, portrays revolution as experienced by worker ranks. Allen's book will stimulate specialists and open up a new world for the general reader." —John Riddell

"This short but invaluable book shows us the Russian Revolution not from the top, not from the bottom, but from the middle: from the party activists who wrote leaflets addressed to the workers the Bolsheviks needed to convince. The slogans come alive in these eloquent evocations of the Bolshevik message. Barbara Allen provides us with all we need to know in order to hear the impassioned voices of 1917." —Lars T. Lih

LEAFLETS
OF THE
RUSSIAN
REVOLUTION

SOCIALIST ORGANIZING IN 1917

Edited and Translated by
Barbara C. Allen

Haymarket Books
Chicago, Illinois

Published by
Haymarket Books
P.O. Box 180165
Chicago, IL 60618
773-583-7884
info@haymarketbooks.org
www.haymarketbooks.org

ISBN: 978-1-60846-970-3

Trade distribution:
In the US, Consortium Book Sales and Distribution, www.cbsd.com
In Canada, Publishers Group Canada, www.pgcbooks.ca
In the UK, Turnaround Publisher Services, www.turnaround-uk.com
All other countries, Ingram Publisher Services International, intlsales@
perseusbooks.com

This book was published with the generous support of the Wallace Action
Fund and Lannan Foundation.

Cover design by Jamie Kerry. Cover image from a poster by by V. M.
Briskin, reading, "The press is a weapon of the Proletariat!"

Printed in the United States.

Library of Congress CIP Data is available.

10 9 8 7 6 5 4 3 2 1

*To my sister Patricia Allen Rogers and all
the other reference librarians*

CONTENTS

PREFACE

This book began as a compilation of leaflet translations I published in a series, *1917: The View from the Streets*, edited by John Riddell and copublished on his blog and the SocialistWorker.org website. The leaflet translations published here in part II feature some corrections and addenda to those published in the series. To contextualize the collection, I have added an introductory essay (part I) about the events of 1917 in Russia.

The leaflets represent the perspectives of socialist political parties and soviets; to round out these activist viewpoints, I have included additional documents from other forms of leftist worker organizations that convey the political and economic struggle for the improvement of workers' lives. Part III offers several translations of key documents about organizing armed worker militias. Part IV contains selected translations of documents relating to building the Russian Metalworkers' Union. Finally, a document in part V assesses the state of the workers' movement immediately after the Bolshevik seizure of power.

This collection is not meant to be a comprehensive collection of documents representing a broad spectrum of forces and organizations that contributed to events in 1917.[1] Rather, it is intended to foster discussion about the historical roles of socialist parties, trade unions, worker militias, and workers' and soldiers' councils (soviets) in the Russian Revolution. Documents selected for this collection emerge from the Russian Social Democratic Workers' Party (RSDRP) organizations of Bolsheviks and Mensheviks, the Party of Socialist Revolutionaries, the Social Democratic Interdistrict Committee (Mezhraionka), the Petrograd Soviet of Workers' and Soldiers' Deputies, the worker militias and Red Guard, and the Petrograd Union of Metalworkers.

As revolution began, both Bolsheviks and Mensheviks were opposed to imperialist war, but Bolsheviks sought a provisional revolutionary government while Mensheviks called for cooperation with liberals to create a democratic republic led by a provisional government. Distrusting liberals, Bolsheviks warned workers against making common efforts with them. Mezhraionka members wanted to unite the RSDRP Bolshevik and Menshevik factional organizations into a common front against the war and the autocracy. They warned workers not to allow liberals to draw them into patriotic demonstrations and organizations. By summer 2017, Mezhraionka folded into the Bolshevik Party. The Party of Socialist Revolutionaries (SRs) appealed to peasants and workers recently arrived from the countryside with a program calling for agrarian land reform, yet it did not have the centralized hierarchy characteristic of the Marxist RSDRP organizations. Therefore, SRs could be found taking a variety of political stances through 1917. By the end of the year, the party had split into left and right organizations. Left SRs aligned with the Bolsheviks to create a governing coalition after the Bolsheviks came to power. Right SRs and Mensheviks had proven willing to join liberals in the Provisional Government and were opposed to joining a government in which Vladimir Lenin and Leon Trotsky held leading roles.

The soviets represented workers and soldiers who were united in socialist organizations. Until the fall of 1917, the Petrograd Soviet was dominated by moderate socialists like the Mensheviks who did not think the time right to contest bourgeois government rule. Worker militias originated during the February 1917 Revolution to keep order as police forces disintegrated. Bolsheviks and Mensheviks disagreed over whether the worker militias should maintain their original role or be transformed into revolutionary forces. Mensheviks worried about potential conflict between armed worker guards and regular military troops. Bolsheviks came to employ the term "worker guard" to signify a more revolutionary force. By August 1917, "red guards" had superseded worker militias. Mensheviks and other moderate socialists dominated the trade union movement, but unions such as the Metalworkers had parity between Bolsheviks and Mensheviks. Trade union organizers from all socialist factions worked together on practical questions around building unions, but differed on political strategies for taking power.

Throughout 1917, among all socialist organizations there was a great deal of flux in membership and political leanings, especially on the questions of which body or bodies should hold power and of which classes should compose ruling bodies. Moderate and radical positions were fluid in the context of the revolutionary moment. Some individuals who had been moderate were radicalized during the year, while others moved closer to liberal positions. Not only did revolutionaries migrate between moderate and radical views, but they sometimes held moderate and radical positions on different issues at the same time. Moreover, even in the most united groups and factions there were subtle differences in positions on discrete political issues. Finally, many socialists in and outside of trade unions considered themselves independent and free from factionalism.

The presence of Russian metalworker Alexander Shlyapnikov looms large in this collection. The most senior member of the RSDRP (Bolshevik) Central Committee on the scene during the February 1917 Revolution, chair of the Petrograd and All-Russian Metalworkers' Unions, and the first Soviet Commissar of Labor, he was also a respected memoirist of the Russian Revolution, and the leaflets featured in part II, penned by various authors, are taken from the appendices to his memoirs. He also played a key role in drafting many of the other documents included in the collection.

*　*　*

John Riddell helped very much to improve the style of my leaflet translations, for which I am grateful. When I revised the leaflet translations, I paid heed to comments offered by those who read them on Riddell's blog. Librarians at the Russian State Library in Moscow, the Van Pelt Library at the University of Pennsylvania, and La Salle University's Connelly Library helped me work with newspapers. Timofey Rakov of the European University of St. Petersburg aided in photographing some articles. Brill gave permission to include an essay about 1917 in part I and the conclusion, both of which were extracted from my biography of Alexander Shlyapnikov.[2] I am thankful to my copy editor Brian Baughan, Nisha Bolsey, John Mc-Donald, Rachel Cohen, Jamie Kerry, and others in the production team at Haymarket Books. As ever, my deepest gratitude goes to Alexander Rabinowitch for teaching me about the Russian Revolution and how to evaluate sources.

NOTES ABOUT THE TEXT

This book renders dates according to the Julian calendar, which Russia used in 1917. It ran thirteen days behind the Gregorian calendar that was observed in much of the rest of Europe and by the United States, and is in general use today. Russia switched to the Gregorian calendar in 1918.

Also, the book generally follows the Library of Congress system of transliterating Russian Cyrillic into the Latin alphabet, with some exceptions. The letter "y" is usually substituted for "й" or "ий" in proper names. The letter "x" is substituted for "кс." Diacritical marks for the Russian letters "ь" and "ъ" are omitted, except in bibliographical references.

After World War I broke out in 1914, Russia changed the name of its capital city, St. Petersburg, to Petrograd in a linguistic gesture of patriotism. The Bolshevik Petersburg Committee, however, retained the old name as a rebuff of the patriotic, pro-war stance.

PART I

The Revolutionary Year 1917

Three years of total war in 1914–16, with attendant economic crises, exhausted Russian society and discredited Tsar Nicholas II's regime, which fell in February 1917 as a consequence of a mass protest in Petrograd against food and fuel shortages. After tsarist rule in Russia ended, an eight-month contest began between liberals, moderate socialists, and radical leftists over the structure of government in Russia and important questions such as participation in the war and land redistribution. A boisterous range of opinions regarding freedom of speech, the press, and assembly filled newspapers and the streets during 1917. Hopes reigned high that Russia could follow Western Europe in establishing democratic, participatory constitutional government, but fears of anarchy and chaos also loomed large in the face of mounting economic disaster, growing war casualties, a crime wave, the aspirations of minority nationalities for self-rule, and the fragility of the caretaker government that had replaced the tsarist regime. The power of the Provisional Government, which was composed mostly of nominees from the Duma, the weak legislative body that had existed under tsarist rule, was challenged by soviets, which were bodies elected by workers, soldiers, and peasants.

THE FEBRUARY REVOLUTION

The prelude to revolution in Petrograd encompassed an impressive strike of 140,000 workers (40 percent of the city's total worker population) on January 9, 1917, which was the anniversary of the 1905 Bloody Sunday massacre, when a peaceful demonstration of workers in the capital city met lethal reprisals from the tsarist government's

Cossack forces. Workers blamed the war and the monarchy for the intolerable economic hardship. Although the strike's initiators were arrested in late January, the rebellious mood among Petrograd's workers did not dissipate. Workers engaged in labor protests almost constantly from January 9 to February 22, when directors of the Putilov factory, the largest plant in Russia, locked out workers. Then on February 23, International Women's Day, women textile workers, angered by long lines and high prices for bread, initiated an insurrection that brought one hundred thousand workers out on strike. Metalworker activists honed the rhetoric of the protestors' nascent political demands. Soldiers proved reluctant to disperse demonstrators. By the next day, two-thirds of the city's industrial workforce was on strike. On February 25, middle-class citizens and students joined the demonstrations. Workers attacked police, and even some troops began to turn against them. By February 27, soldiers were in full insurrection, crowds had freed political prisoners and criminals from jail, and the police melted away.[3]

During the February Revolution, events moved ahead faster than all socialist parties could anticipate. None expected Women's Day to ignite a revolution. The role of women as a revolutionary catalyst had not been foreseen in the programs and strategies Russian socialists had devised in the nearly two decades prior to the revolution. Russian Social Democrats (SDs), who had organized a party in 1898 and then split into factions in 1903, had a Marxist program based on the inevitability of conflict between labor and capital and the eventual abolition of private property. Bolsheviks wanted only active revolutionaries to be party members, while the Mensheviks allowed that sympathizers could join. The Socialist Revolutionaries (SRs), whose party formed in 1902, expanded the definition of an exploited class to include peasants as well as workers, and exploiters to include noble landowners along with capitalists. They advocated socialization and equal distribution of the land to those who tilled it, while the SDs' agricultural plans were poorly developed. Unlike the SDs, the SRs did not have a central organization. Some of them pursued terrorist tactics. The SRs disagreed with Lenin's view that class divisions had developed among the peasantry. In the underground, many socialists cooperated in their practical work despite the theoretical differences among them.

During the 1917 Revolution, Russian Social Democratic Mensheviks tended toward moderation, while their rivals the Bolsheviks were radical on these questions. Socialist Revolutionaries could be found on both sides of the moderate/radical divide. In addition, individuals changed their positions throughout the year as their interpretations of rapidly fluctuating revolutionary events evolved. While moderate socialists tried to restrain strikes, more radical socialists came out in favor of them. Left socialists cooperated in issuing appeals and organizing events.

Printed leaflets had usually served as signals for mass actions, but issuing revolutionary propaganda was difficult given police harassment. A group of revolutionary Social Democrats called the Interdistrictites (Mezhraionka) was probably the major producer of socialist leaflets during the February Revolution. Bolsheviks in the Vyborg district of Petrograd were among the most radical. They wanted to arm detachments of worker guards, but the most senior representative of the Bolshevik CC in Petrograd, metalworker Alexander Shlyapnikov, refused to authorize this. He argued that worker guards could not stand up against trained military forces. Therefore, in his opinion, it was crucial for workers to win over military units. Indeed, it appeared by February 27 that the revolution could descend into chaotic violence.[4]

The February Revolution culminated on February 27. Tsarist ministers resigned. Socialists formed the Petrograd Soviet of Workers' and Soldiers' Deputies, a citywide electoral body representing workers and soldiers through political parties and other organizations; its leading body was an Executive Committee. Liberal leaders of the Duma decided to create a temporary government. When, under pressure, Tsar Nicholas II abdicated on behalf of himself and his son on March 2, 1917, power quickly devolved to the Provisional Government, which was created on the same day by agreement between the leaders of the Duma and the Petrograd Soviet. Prince Georgy Lvov, a liberal landowner, was its head. Alexander Kerensky, a pro-war socialist, joined the new government as minister of justice, later becoming minister of war. Moderate and radical socialists (Mensheviks, SRs, Bolsheviks, and unaffiliated socialists) cooperated in creating the Petrograd Soviet. Soviets would form in many Russian cities. Within large cities, there were district soviets. Although a majority of the Soviet Executive Committee had agreed to support the Provisional Government, this was the position of moderate Mensheviks and SRs who regarded the February Revolution as "bourgeois." They believed it unrealistic and contrary to Marxist theory to oppose the creation of a bourgeois government. Radical socialists such as the Bolsheviks were less willing to give the bourgeoisie the opportunity to consolidate its power.[5]

The monarchist right having withered as tsarism collapsed, the political spectrum ranged from moderate right to far left. Centrist non-socialists, who were mostly liberal, cooperated with moderate socialists during the interval between the two 1917 revolutions of February and October. The most important liberal party was the Constitutional Democrats [Kadets]; their most prominent spokesman, Pavel Milyukov, became minister of foreign affairs. Liberals desired to protect Russia from German conquest, resolve the economic crisis, create peace among social groups, and prepare elections based on universal suffrage for a Constituent Assembly that would organize a new constitutional government for Russia. Many civic organizations had a liberal bent; these were organized by professionals for political, educational, and cultural causes. As the crisis deepened, those who had seemed liberal came to be perceived as conservative.[6]

A range of opinions existed among Petrograd Bolsheviks over their stance toward the Provisional Government. Lenin's views were outlined in his "Letters from Afar," which he wrote in early March 1917 while still in Switzerland. These consisted of opposition to the Provisional Government, a call for Soviet rule, and opposition to the war. Most Bolsheviks in Petrograd agreed with Lenin's call for an end to the war, but their opinions varied widely on whether to cooperate with the Provisional Government. A majority of the Petersburg Committee (which did not change its name after war began) advocated non-opposition to the Provisional Government, in line with the resolution adopted by the Petrograd Soviet. The far-left Vyborg District Bolshevik Committee called on workers to seize power.[7]

Like Lenin, the members of the Russian Bureau of the RSDRP(b) (Russian Social Democratic Workers' Party [Bolsheviks]) Central Committee (Alexander Shlyapnikov, Vyacheslav Molotov, and Peter Zalutsky) opposed the Provisional Government and called for the Soviet to form a provisional revolutionary government, which would have had an agenda of ending the war, establishing a democratic republic, securing the eight-hour work day, confiscating landowners' estates, supplying the army and urban population with food, and calling a Constituent Assembly.[8] Nevertheless, the Russian Bureau members, who all were in Petrograd, realized perhaps better than Lenin that they needed to cooperate with other left socialists.

The Russian Bureau membership expanded throughout March as Bolshevik leaders returned from prison or exile. Of these, Lev Kamenev was the most prominent. He led the moderate Bolsheviks, who included Joseph Stalin; these Bolsheviks were closer to the Petrograd Soviet majority's assessment of the Provisional Government than they were to Lenin's views. They claimed authority in the name of the former Bolshevik Duma delegation. The CC Russian Bureau struggled ineffectively with the moderate Bolsheviks. Although the Bureau at first rejected Kamenev as a member, he circumvented it by taking control of the Bolshevik newspaper, *Pravda*. Kamenev's group also outmaneuvered the Russian Bureau on the floor of the Soviet by supporting moderate positions in the name of the Bolshevik Party. Unwilling to reveal disunity, Russian Bureau members did not speak.[9]

When Kamenev's March 15 *Pravda* editorial supported continuing the war, consternation ensued among Bolshevik activists. The methods of the moderates, forcing through their own views without consulting rank-and-file members, were as much at issue as their policies. Further, the content of *Pravda* was not so blatantly defensist, but it still did not publish a large part of Lenin's letters. Moreover, by March 18, Kamenev had persuaded the Petersburg Committee to vote for "conditional support" for the Provisional Government.[10]

When Lenin arrived in Petrograd via train across Germany, Sweden, and Finland, the Mensheviks and Kamenev's Bolsheviks appeared to be on the verge of reunification. Lenin immediately and emphatically expressed his disagreement with Bolshevik moderates' positions on the war and toward the Provisional Government. His *April Theses* called for the transformation of world war into international proletarian revolution, for opposition to the Provisional Government, and for a total rejection of any efforts to heal the schism among Russian Social Democrats. Lenin placed priority on "a struggle for transfer of all power to the Soviets," control over which he hoped soon to wrest from the moderate socialists. Nevertheless, he did not endorse the radical Bolsheviks' appeals for an immediate seizure of power. He realized that more preparation was necessary before attempting to bring down the Provisional Government. Initially, most Bolsheviks rejected Lenin's positions, but this soon changed.[11]

Foreign Minister Milyukov, in assuring the Allies in an April 20 telegram that Russia would wage war according to the tsarist government's treaties with them, radicalized many leftists. By the Bolsheviks' Seventh Party Conference (April 24–29, 1917), a large majority of delegates agreed with Lenin's positions on the Provisional Government and the war. Nevertheless, the conference did not agree wholly with his claim that Russia was undergoing a transition to socialist revolution, but leaned somewhat toward Kamenev's position that Russia was still in the process of a bourgeois-liberal revolution.[12]

WORKERS' MILITIA AND RED GUARD

During the February Revolution, only the police forces had backed the tsarist government out of all the forces of order that had helped the regime survive the 1905 Revolution. All over Russia in the wake of the tsarist regime's downfall, tsarist police forces disintegrated. Local militias replaced them, with varying degrees of effectiveness as crime spiraled out of control through the year. The Petrograd Soviet officially created the worker militia of Petrograd on February

28, 1917, with the Soviet assigning Bolshevik Alexander Shlyapnikov the task of overseeing the arming and organization of the
militia. In spring and summer 1917, the Petrograd worker militias
were superseded by the Red Guard, which in late August played
an important role in defeating General Lavr Kornilov's attempts at
counterrevolution.[13]

The extent of the militia's responsibilities were a sensitive
question, as casting them too much in terms of class conflict could
provoke opposition from the non-worker social milieu. Shlyapnikov
saw the purpose of the workers' militia as not only to police factory
districts, but also to defend gains made for workers during the February Revolution. He revealed this to a March 5 meeting dedicated
to forming a civil militia under the Petrograd city administration.
The Soviet sent him to the meeting as its representative. He spoke
there of the need to broaden the militia's responsibilities to prevent
a restoration of the monarchy and "to ease the movement of the
revolution forward." This was his own opinion; the Soviet had not
taken a stance. In late April 1917, the Soviet, Provisional Government, and city administration agreed that worker militias should
unite with the civil militia of Petrograd, but many units continued to
exist independently of the civil militia.[14]

When the Petrograd Soviet created a section on militia affairs in
mid-March, it removed from Shlyapnikov formal responsibility for
links with militias. In late March and early April, he began to advocate a worker "guard." Shlyapnikov and Konstantin Eremeev, who
in December 1917 became Petrograd military district commander,
decided to organize the guard in the most "revolutionary" worker
districts. Shlyapnikov authored the Vyborg District Soviet's April
29 decree on the organization of the workers' guard. The Vyborg
regulations restricted membership in the guard to workers who belonged to a socialist party or a trade union, or who were chosen by
their fellow factory workers. The regulations defined the main tasks
of the workers' guard as: "1) struggle with the counterrevolution, 2)
armed defense of the working class and 3) defense of all citizens' life
and safety." Other districts modeled their Red Guard units on those
of Vyborg. In August 1917, the Red Guard central staff was formed.[15]

When revolutionary socialists began organizing the Red Guard, moderate socialists and liberals feared that the Bolsheviks would use the guard for partisan purposes. Defending the Red Guard against these charges, Shlyapnikov explained that it was necessary for several reasons. First, when the war ended, the radicalized Petrograd garrison would depart the capital, leaving workers vulnerable to repression by the Provisional Government and police. Second, the professional militia was "cut off" from the people and had its own institutional interests. Workers therefore required their own militia, which would guard their interests. All guard units would be under the direction of their district soviets, which would eliminate any threat of spontaneous or independent action. Finally, workers would arm themselves no matter what. To avoid "disorder," the soviets and parties should cooperate in forming a network of militias under the control of the soviets.[16]

ORGANIZING THE PETROGRAD METALWORKERS' UNION

Despite a high level of activism, metalworkers were among the last industrial workers to form a citywide union in 1917. Reasons for this included the competing priorities of individual metalworkers' political activism, such as leading demonstrations and organizing soviets; the prominence in metalworking factories of elected factory committees, which had a stronger tradition in Russia as forms of workers' organization than did trade unions; and the strong craft loyalty of many skilled workers, which made membership in a craft union more attractive than membership in a union of the industry in which they were employed. Finally, "district patriotism" motivated some metalworkers, who worried that a central leadership could be less responsive than district-level leaders.[17]

Finally, on April 23, 1917, a constituent assembly of Petrograd district level metalworker union representatives formally approved the Petrograd Metalworkers' Union's statutes. On May 7, a citywide delegates' council elected a central board composed of an unaffiliated socialist, Alexei Gastev; a Menshevik, I. G. Volkov; and Shlyapnikov. The first session of the central committee of the Petrograd

Metalworkers' Union met on May 27. By June 11, union leaders had begun to register the unemployed in labor exchanges and to find work for them. They had also set up a journal called *Metallist*. More importantly, they had begun to mediate conflicts between workers and industrialists, which was a major step toward boosting workers' confidence in the efficacy of a union.[18]

The work of the Petrograd Metalworkers' Union laid the foundation for the All-Russian Metalworkers' Union, which worker delegates from across Russia formed in late June/early July 1917.[19] Delegates elected four Bolsheviks and four Mensheviks to its central committee. A Bolshevik (Shlyapnikov) and a Menshevik (Volkov) tied for the largest number of votes. Gastev, the ninth member, soon aligned himself with the Bolsheviks.[20] Shlyapnikov was elected chair at the first meeting of the central committee, on June 29, 1917, perhaps due to Gastev's swing vote. Aside from making the Petrograd journal *Metallist* the all-Russian organ of the union, the committee could do little else at that time. All-Russian union leaders attended regional metalworker conferences, conferences of workers in the artillery department, and soviet meetings; advised regional unions on organizing; and distributed literature to regional unions. Several members returned to work in their provincial unions. Those remaining in Petrograd became absorbed in wage rates negotiations. Before the All-Russian Metalworkers' Union could fully function, many local problems had to be resolved, including the rivalry for members between the unions and factory committees.[21]

Moderate union leaders, including Bolsheviks and Mensheviks, favored the subordination of factory committees to industrial unions at the factory level. Bolshevik radicals, on the other hand, advocated an independent role for the committees. At the First Conference of the Petrograd Factory Committees, held May 30–June 5, 1917, radical Bolsheviks won approval of a central council for the factory committees, thus unifying the factory-committee movement. Alarmed moderates saw this as a threat to trade unions, but the radicals held a stronger position. The radicals conceded that the Central Council of Factory Committees should coordinate its actions with the All-Russian Central Trade Union Council (VTsSPS), but there was no indication of any subordinate relationship. In addition, some moderate Bolsheviks won election to the Central Council of Factory Committees.[22]

The Metalworkers' Union did not accept the principle of factory-committee independence and quickly asserted that the trade union was to take priority over the factory committee in responsibility for workers' conduct. Furthermore, it declared that only the union could represent workers in negotiations with factory owners and the state, and in matters relating to workers' control ("control" usually meant "supervision" of factory operations and working conditions, but the definition was not static, sometimes tending toward the more ambitious concept of worker administration of factories). Finally, it called for the complete subordination of the factory committees to the unions, which was a direct challenge to the authority of the Central Council of Factory Committees. Nevertheless, until the formal subjugation of factory committees to trade unions in early 1918, trade unions and factory committees continued to follow divergent policies.[23]

In the face of so many factors dividing metalworkers, Metalworkers' Union leaders searched for something to unite them. They found this in the struggle for a system of wage rates for all categories of workers, upon which union leaders and industrialists would agree. This would address workers' dissatisfaction with working conditions and wages.[24] Factory committees had begun the fight for higher wages, but union representatives decided that a uniform standard was necessary. Uncoordinated efforts to achieve higher wages were paralyzing and were fragmenting the labor movement. The union sought to create a more rational system of pay and working hours, to increase wages for unskilled workers, oversee hiring and firing decisions, and "establish a procedure for the arbitration of disputes." The wage rates negotiations and agreement proved to be the most successful means of uniting metalworkers around their union, attracting workers away from factory committees and craft-based unions and building a strong organization.[25]

Some Metalworkers' Union leaders, including the chair Shlyapnikov, had worked in West European factories and were well-informed about wage rates agreements already in place in Western industry.[26]

Having formed a commission to study wage rates, they decided to propose rates based on the minimum cost of living, on professional qualifications, the difficulty and complexity of work, and the danger of working conditions. With no pre-existing collections of statistics to guide them, commission members collected statistics on their own, factory-by-factory, and determined prices of essential groceries and goods. The union's contract categorized workers according to skill level and length of work experience.[27]

Before settling on a rates system, the trade union leadership's commission had to agree with leaders of unskilled metalworkers, who were especially militant in the spring of 1917. Their already low wages devastated by inflation in spring 1917, unskilled metalworkers formed their own union in early April to press for wage increases. In June 1917, they joined the Metalworkers' Union for greater negotiating leverage. In early June, the unskilled metalworkers of Vyborg district presented their wage demands to the leadership of the Metalworkers' Union. A strike of unskilled workers at the Putilov works briefly disrupted negotiations between union leaders and the unskilled, but also gave teeth to union demands in negotiations with factory owners.[28] Petrograd Metalworkers' Union leaders entered wage rates negotiations with the Society of Factory Owners and Manufacturers on June 22. The Metals Department of the Provisional Government's Ministry of Labor (created in May 1917) mediated. Union leaders and representatives of the factory owners soon came to an initial agreement, but on June 25 the citywide delegates' council of the Petrograd Metalworkers' Union presented obstacles to a compromise. Although the delegates' assembly approved "guiding principles" for the wage rates agreement, it rejected all minimum-pay rates proposed by the Society of Factory Owners. Shlyapnikov believed that the great difference between the factory owners' proposed rates for the unskilled and for apprentices made a compromise difficult. Delegates especially objected fiercely to the factory owners' proposal that workers maintain a certain level of productivity to receive wages according to wage rates in the agreement.[29]

Shlyapnikov justified the guarantee of productivity by explaining that its acceptance gained credibility for the union in the eyes of "bourgeois" society and the state, because it undermined capitalists' claims that workers wanted a guaranteed minimum wage without a guaranteed minimum of labor input. To allay the concerns of union delegates, the union's negotiators replaced the provision guaranteeing productivity with a provision on output norms, perhaps only a semantic difference. Before presenting the norms resolution to the delegates' assembly, Shlyapnikov had it approved not only by the Metalworkers' Union central board, but also by all district boards and representatives of the Soviet and the political parties represented within it. Finally, union leaders threatened to resign if delegates did not cooperate. A delegates' assembly on July 2 caved in to their leaders' pressure and accepted the guarantee of productivity. Nevertheless, delegates made the caveat that such a guarantee made obligatory future discussion of implementing workers' control of production, which in their opinion was the only way to guarantee "both labor productivity and the productivity of the enterprise as a whole."[30] With the successful compromise, union negotiators calculated that they would soon agree with factory owners. On the next day, however, an abortive radical socialist uprising intervened, increasing friction between workers and industrialists and disrupting the wage rates negotiators' timetable.

THE JULY DAYS

In spring 1917, Russian military and political leaders prepared the last major Russian military offensive of World War I, aiming to force back German and Austrian forces, reinvigorate the morale of Russian troops, and strengthen Russia's negotiating position in future peace talks. Conservatives, liberals, and moderate socialists supported it, while Bolsheviks and Left SRs opposed it. Fearing high casualties, soldiers and workers believed the government should prioritize addressing economic problems over continuing the war. Their dissatisfaction was expressed in the protests of the "June Days" in Petrograd, which culminated in a June 18 demonstration of nearly half a million people, most of them against the war. The offensive began impressively in Galicia that same day, but Russian troops soon fell back under the onslaught of a German counteroffensive.[31] The imminent collapse of the offensive, accompanied by a sharpened crisis in Petrograd's food and fuel supply, brought about a crisis of confidence in the government, which itself was in crisis after the July 2 resignation of Kadet ministers who opposed Ukrainian autonomy. The result was the July Uprising ("July Days").

Both workers and soldiers played important roles in the uprising. Unrest in each group fed dissatisfaction in the other. Soldiers, who feared being transferred to the front, began the uprising on July 3. Members of the Bolshevik Military Organization assisted the soldiers, despite the Bolshevik Party CC's orders to the contrary. Anarchists and Left SRs encouraged the soldiers. Workers, disgruntled over low wages and already on strike, joined the demonstrations.

Despite the Soviet's condemnation, and the Bolshevik CC's opposition, soldiers and workers marched on the Tauride Palace, where the Soviet met. Workers and soldiers demonstrated around Tauride Palace through the night of July 3 and the morning of July 4. After tens of thousands of demonstrators surrounded the palace, the Bolshevik CC gave its support to the demonstrations and called for all power to the soviets. The Soviet majority, however, did not waver in its opposition to the uprising. As quickly as they had begun, the demonstrations subsided. This was due to 1) the Provisional Government's success in painting the Bolsheviks as German-sponsored saboteurs of the Russian war effort; 2) an upsurge in violence associated with the demonstrations; and 3) news that loyal troops were on their way to Petrograd. The government quickly shut down *Pravda*, evicted the Bolsheviks from their party headquarters, and arrested many of their leaders. Lenin escaped arrest by going underground and fleeing in disguise to Finland in August.[32]

When the Provisional Government mustered loyal troops and cracked down on the Bolsheviks, trade unions were also in the line of fire. A military patrol raided the central offices of the Metalworkers' Union on the Fontanka embankment, but the union was not shut down. The Trud publishing house, which printed much material for the Metalworkers' Union, was closed and some of its staff arrested. Its closure delayed by at least a month the publication of the first issue of the union's journal, *Metallist*. Bolshevik Party headquarters at the former mansion of ballerina Mathilde Kshesinskaya (Tsar Nicholas II's former lover) was looted, vandalized, and occupied by pro-government soldiers. Bolshevik trade union leaders arranged for trade-union and factory-committee leaders to denounce the allegations against Bolshevik leaders of having been German agents.[33] Nevertheless, the popular mood had turned against the Bolsheviks.

TRADE-UNIONIST AGENDA

The abortive July Uprising derailed wage rates negotiations. By the time negotiations restarted on July 12, the Society of Factory Owners, emboldened by the government's success in crushing the uprising, had decided not to compromise. The worsening economic crisis also hardened the industrialists' negotiating stance, as they feared that wage guarantees could threaten the survival of their businesses. Thus, the factory owners replaced "liberal" negotiators with more conservative ones, who contested norms of wages by groups and categories. The industrialists' objection to rates was especially adamant in relation to unskilled workers, who made up the largest portion of the workforce.[34]

Unable to agree on rates, union leaders and factory owners appealed to the Ministry of Labor to mediate. The Metalworkers' Union, under enormous pressure from unskilled members, prepared for a general strike of all workers in the industry. Union leaders took this step against the advice of Bolshevik Party leaders, who feared it was too extreme a step so soon after the July Days. On July 22, the Ministry of Labor assigned wage rates to the unskilled and semi-skilled, which were less than what the union demanded, but more than what the factory owners offered. When the Society of Factory Owners refused to comply, an assembly of union delegates called a general strike. In response, the Ministry of Labor declared that it would compel factory owners to comply with the government's decision. Finding the Labor Ministry's offer acceptable, union leaders persuaded delegates to cancel their strike and to accept the offer as the best possible under existing conditions. Delegates expressed their dissatisfaction, however, in their final resolution, which stated that the workers' plight could only ultimately be resolved by social and economic legislation, the state regulation of industry, and immediate peace. These preconditions, they believed, could only be fulfilled by a revolution that would bring workers to power. The Petrograd Metalworkers' Union and the Society of Factory Owners signed the wage rates agreement on August 7, 1917.[35]

The Russian trade union leaders' successful negotiation of a wage rates agreement during the revolutionary year 1917 was a remarkable achievement, even though inflation and the high cost of living rapidly outpaced its norms. It was a major accomplishment of the Metalworkers' Union to put the agreement into force in most Petrograd factories by October 1917, when the industrial economy was in complete crisis. Union leaders knew that Russian economic conditions in 1917 made the wage rates agreement of limited immediate use and that it had not addressed the exploitative relationship between capitalist and worker. On the other hand, they saw in it a step toward unity for workers, for it set a standard and ceased the practice of pitting workers against one another. Once the agreement was in place, increases in rates could be negotiated. Unions and factory committees would cooperate in forming a rate commission, which would represent each major shop within the factory. All representatives had to be union members and had to be responsible both to their electorate and to the union, a provision that gave unions precedence over factory committees. If workers disapproved of their elected representatives' actions, they would present their grievances to the union rather than unilaterally recall representatives.[36] Commission members would be accountable both to their worker electorate and to union leaders.

The wage rates negotiations were only one way of strengthening the Russian unions. Another was absorbing craft unions into industrial unions, which had a potentially broader base and were more relevant to an industry composed mostly of large factories. Many union leaders called for the amalgamation of craft-based unions into industrial unions. Neither highly qualified nor unskilled metalworkers objected to their integration into a production union.

Both groups readily agreed to present their grievances to the union for arbitration. Craft-based unions' failure to join the industrial union greatly hindered its attempts to carry out negotiations or strikes involving all occupations in the metalworking industry.[37] The Petrograd Metalworkers' Union absorbed more than twenty craft-based unions in early 1917, but faced strong resistance from several groups. The more troublesome targets of unionization included craftsmen with a strong guild mentality, such as stokers, welders, pattern makers, and woodworkers, all of whom worked in the metals, textile, and leather industries. Much of union leaders' work in 1917 involved persuading, pressuring, or coercing reluctant craft-based unions to join the industrial union. Union leaders' rationale for this was that it was counterproductive for several different unions to exist in the same factory, because independent actions of craft-based unions had harmed other workers. To achieve their goals, the craftspeople needed the leverage created by the support of other workers. Crafts workers were offered the concession of a measure of autonomy through profession-based commissions once they joined the union.[38] Compared to other countries, Russia made great strides toward industrial unionism in 1917.[39] Both the wage rates negotiations and the absorption of craft unions brought many new workers into unions. The Petrograd Metalworkers' Union membership went from 70,000 in June to more than 140,000 by October, perhaps even 190,000 (between one-third and one-half of all trade union members in Petrograd).[40]

Another very contentious issue that faced trade-union leaders was whether unions should take a stand on political questions, a conflict that also divided trade unionists outside of Russia. "Internationalists" favored intervention in political issues that affected workers' lives, such as the World War, while "neutralists" believed that unions should limit themselves strictly to economic questions, such as pay rates and the length of the working day. Most Bolsheviks favored politicizing the trade unions, which meant taking a stance against the war and against cooperation with liberals and for a world socialist revolution. Many Mensheviks were "neutralists," fearing that involvement in politics would weaken the unions' ability to fight for the workers' economic rights. SRs could be found on both sides. Some neutralists thought that trade unions should push for greater social and political democracy, but that unions should not take stands on individual political questions. Most Menshevik trade unionists did not want unions to advocate the transfer of all power to the soviets, while most Bolsheviks did. In 1917, many Mensheviks and SRs worked within various unions. But many positions were in flux in 1917 and individuals switched positions and even parties during that year.[41]

In late September, work began on an all-Russian wage rates agreement and on a plan for workers' control of industrial enterprises. The union's plan presented financial control to the highest regulatory government institutions and called for a factory technical assembly to provide technical and administrative leadership of the enterprise. The assembly would consist of workers' representatives, technical supervisors, and commercial managers of the factory. Union leaders also intended to push for union representatives to join state economic regulatory institutions. They resolved (on October 13) to convoke a constituent congress in Petrograd or Moscow at the end of November.[42] But the October Revolution intervened, substantially altering the trade unionists' agenda.

BOLSHEVIKS COME TO POWER

The Bolshevik Party had been hit hard by government repression and quite a bit of popular disapproval after the failed July Uprising, for which it was blamed. The Bolsheviks' opportunity for recovery came in late August 1917. Over the summer, the Provisional Government underwent a change in composition, losing some liberals and gaining socialists. Kerensky became prime minister. Yet strong political differences among parties represented in the government contributed to its increasing inability to stop the spiraling trend toward chaos in Russia. Those on the right reasserted themselves, seeking a strong man to restore order. They believed they had found him in General Lavr Kornilov, a Cossack with a heroic reputation but a weak comprehension of politics. The government's restoration of the death penalty in the army and measures to crush worker and peasant initiative were viewed by the radical left as ominous forebodings of counterrevolution. Even some liberals began to move toward the right. Meanwhile, the general population seemed to be radicalizing in a leftward direction. On August 27–31, the Kornilov Affair marked a watershed moment in 1917 politics, as an effort by Kerensky and Kornilov to prepare martial law in Petrograd collapsed in mutual suspicion. The Soviet, the socialist parties, the Red Guards, and the railway workers cooperated to prevent what they perceived as an attempted coup by Kornilov. Kerensky was discredited, but the Bolsheviks were redeemed, along with the rest of the radical left.[43]

The popular mood had grown more radical in Russia over the summer. A peasant rebellion had gathered steam, as state power in the countryside dissipated and peasants seized control of land that they had long desired. Socialist Revolutionaries had established peasant soviets, but peasants often acted through land committees they constituted themselves and grew increasingly frustrated with the Provisional Government's hesitation to implement land reform. Along the borderlands, minority nationalities that at first had sought autonomy increasingly began to seek independence from the collapsing Russian Empire. While liberals and moderate socialists were reluctant to accommodate national self-determination, Lenin's already developed stance on national autonomy allowed Bolsheviks and other radical leftists to ally with minority nationalists. Worker discontent grew over factory closings and, as the supply crisis grew sharper, urban residents generally struggled to feed themselves and heat their homes.[44]

Lenin and other radical Bolsheviks began to urge an armed insurrection to wrest control from the Provisional Government. Moderate Bolsheviks, on the other hand, called for the transfer of power to a government formed from socialist parties represented in the Soviet. Fears were growing among government officials, and in other parties, of a Bolshevik-led insurrection that would result in a dictatorship. The radicals' attempts were initially rebuffed within the Bolshevik Party. In late September 1917, the Bolshevik CC held a strategic session at which its members dismissed Lenin's proposal for a mass uprising. Moderates, as well as those leftists sympathetic to Lenin's appeals, were aware that the Bolshevik Party did not have enough influence among Russian industrial workers to rouse them to insurrection. They also felt that Lenin did not appreciate the workers' deep desire for a revolutionary, but broad-based and democratic, government founded on the soviets. Finally, they saw Lenin's plan as unwarranted in its desperation. There was no immediate threat from the right. Moderates looked to the October Congress of Soviets to take power in the name of all socialist parties in the Soviet.[45]

In late September and early October, Lenin cajoled and bullied to get his way, arguing that the European proletariat was on the verge of revolution, the initiation of which depended on Bolsheviks taking power in Russia. Gathering behind him more militant Bolsheviks who composed a majority in the Petersburg Committee, he revealed to them that the CC had censored his articles in late September, cutting the most radical parts. This revelation brought even the holdouts to his side in sympathy. Radical Bolsheviks gained more support when they accused the Provisional Government of planning to surrender Petrograd to the Germans and thereby "crush" Russia's revolutionary center. By the time Bolshevik leaders met on October 10, Kamenev and Grigory Zinoviev were the only two moderates who voted against Lenin. The CC voted 10–2 to organize an armed uprising. Some moderates such as Alexei Rykov and Victor Nogin, who would have supported Zinoviev and Kamenev, were not present. Shlyapnikov was in Moscow in early October, attending the Moscow Oblast Metalworkers' Union Conference. There he heard metalworkers demand, with immediacy in their tone, soviet power, nationalization of large industry and transport, and the implementation of workers' control (supervision) over production.[46]

Moderate parties began to get wind of Bolshevik intentions, and newspapers began warning of a Bolshevik coup attempt. On October 16, there was a meeting of Bolsheviks from all revolutionary organizations—the Petersburg Committee, the CC, the Bolshevik Military Organization, the Petrograd Soviet, the trade unions, and the factory shops. They were divided over whether and when to seize power. Many participants, including trade union leaders, spoke of a lack of resources and a lack of commitment by workers and soldiers to exclusive Bolshevik rule.[47] A significant minority of those who voted on October 16 were unwilling to approve an "immediate insurrection." Lenin and the Bolshevik Military Organization wanted to make the government takeover an accomplished fact before the Second Congress of Soviets began on October 25.

Events proceeded quickly. Having won over the garrison on the night of October 21–22, on the next day the Bolsheviks organized large demonstrations at which their speakers warned of surrender of the city to the Germans. On October 24, Kerensky closed Bolshevik printing presses. Leon Trotsky responded by calling the Bolshevik Military Revolutionary Committee (MRC), formed on October 20, to arms. Bolshevik trade union leaders participated in the party's seizure of power. Among their activities were organizing fighting and medical brigades, gathering weapons for the Red Guard, and collecting barbed wire for defense of the approaches to Petrograd. Trade union leaders had found the Ministry of Labor unable or unwilling to enforce the unions' agreements with industrialists and they hoped that soviet power would "end political and economic instability and . . . enhance the unions' economic role."[48]

By the morning of October 25, the Military Revolutionary Committee and troops loyal to the left had won major strategic points in the city. Kerensky fled the capital for the city of Pskov to rendezvous with loyal troops and prepare a counteroffensive. When the Congress of Soviets opened late in the evening on October 25, the Bolsheviks had the largest representation, but to form a majority they had to ally with Left SRs. Incensed by the Bolsheviks' coup, the Mensheviks and SRs withdrew from the Congress, leaving the Bolsheviks free to form a government, which moderate socialists did not think would last. Early on the morning of October 26, Bolshevik forces seized the Winter Palace and arrested the government ministers meeting there. On October 27, the Congress of Soviets confirmed the Council of People's Commissars (Sovnarkom), which replaced the old cabinet of ministers. Few of the commissars, however, could claim a proletarian or peasant background.[49]

PART II

The Political Struggle: Leaflets of
Russian Socialist Parties and Soviets

LEAFLET 1
"To the Revolutionary Students of Russia"
December 1916

In December 1916, an organizing committee of Bolshevik-influenced students issued this underground proclamation calling on students in Russia who were opposed to the war to come together with workers and peasants to put a provisional revolutionary government in power. The organizing committee linked revolutionary student circles at higher educational institutions in Petrograd, Russia. Its proclamation reflects the impact of the Zimmerwald movement on leading student revolutionary activists in Russia. European socialists had met during a September 1915 conference in Zimmerwald, Switzerland, where they issued a manifesto condemning World War I as an imperialist war pursued for the sake of capitalist profits. The Zimmerwald Left consisted of socialists who actively supported struggling against the war.[50]

* * *

"Proletarians of all countries, unite!"

> To the revolutionary students of Russia.
> The glory of victory is given only to the brave,
> The fallen in struggle do not know shame . . .
> Youth, our song is sung to you—
> Eternal glory to you."[51]

Comrades! During the years of reaction, when work was difficult and routine, there were no questions demanding definite actions toward their solution. Therefore, the differentiation which was occurring among our students could not come to light in a sufficiently well-defined way. Vulgar, bourgeois moods grew among students and became stronger in the stinking decay of a bastardized constitution. Only now these moods have been revealed in all their strength. Such moods attest to the complete ideological bankruptcy and reckless opportunism of the general student body.

At one time, they seemed united in their revolutionary democratic mood. Now, given the exacerbation of class contradictions in society, students have split into two opposing groups. First, the bourgeois-opportunist group, which is ideologically connected to the Russian liberal bourgeoisie, has become much stronger recently. The second group is revolutionary-socialist and possesses the internationalist, class-based ideology of the world proletariat.

With no desire at all to appeal to the former group, we appeal to those comrades who share our convictions but who for some reason still stand on the sidelines of the socialist work of proletarian organizations. In the past, a large part of the student body merely sympathized with this work, but at the present moment the revolutionary worldview obligates one to take corresponding action. Events force upon these students the need either to renounce their sympathy and to completely merge with the bourgeois sector of students and with the Russian bourgeoisie, or to move from thoughts and words toward definite revolutionary action and to connect themselves with the proletariat in the great struggle to overthrow modern-day slavery.

Yes, the students were very "sympathetic." They talked very much about the interests of "the people," but they spent too much time in thought to be capable of doing the slightest thing in the name of their great values. All the best ones perished. Merging their sense of consciousness and will with those of "the hungry and the slaves," they went forward on the straight path of difficult, heroic struggle against the current Tsar's predatory pack of hounds.

> Eternal memory to those who were lost for the sacred cause!
> Eternal memory to those who were tormented in rotten prisons!
> Eternal memory to those who told us the living word![52]

And the students?! They convinced themselves that they held a definite ideological position and by it they justified their inaction and weak will. They did not notice that they had long ago lost any defined "position." They stood not on the firm foundation of ideological-social convictions, but in a dirty swamp of vulgar opportunism. So they lived for a long time. They breathed the poisoned air of ideological demoralization. They held forth, in their own self-importance, about their highly elevated "position" and the absolute worth of their (stagnant) moods. Years passed by while the students bogged down more and more deeply.

The world war broke out as a result of the plundering policy of the ruling classes and their governments, and it put on the agenda very acute questions, which everyone had to answer quickly. Various social strata in Russia reacted differently to these burning questions and to the terrible events which were unfolding. Up to this time, there was not and could not have been a single attitude among students to these questions. No matter how much the bourgeois press lied about "national unity," the people (proletariat and peasantry) have not wanted war.

The *revolutionary* minority of our students has gone along with the people, not with so-called "society." The students were with the people on the barricades of the first revolution [in 1905], suffered with them during the difficult years of reaction, and along with them tried to prevent the bloody feud of the bourgeoisie, for whom the people are only a means to an end. Together with the proletariat, the students defended the red flag of the International from concerted attack by the bourgeoisie of all countries and by some early teachers of socialism. It is true that chauvinism fooled some students, who actively accepted war and flung themselves into slaughtering imaginary oppressors to defend the "fatherland," meaning the state, and its money bags, which are its heart and soul.

Among those who, from the moment the world slaughter began, did not find anything better to do than merely "not to oppose," there were even some who had said earlier that the state is the most acute expression of class rule and that the current government expresses bourgeois rule. They had considered the only just war to be the war of the proletariat against the bourgeoisie and against the tyranny of Nicholas the Bloody, and the war of actual slaves against actual oppressors.

By their decision "not to oppose," they cut themselves off from most of their comrades. They turned their backs on the proletarian and turned toward dissolution and debauchery. Only after twenty-eight months of war have they now come to recognize with horror that their hands, which they raised as if to defend oppressed peoples, had been woven into a horrible fraternal embrace with tsarism. They feel that they have been deceived and that fraternization with monarchs is the chief reason for long, protracted war without end.

The Second International was not fit to play the role of a revolutionary organization of action even in peacetime, when contradictions between internationalist and national-socialist elements were not so acute. Its majority was unaware of the need for immediate revolutionary acts in case of imperialist war. When world war began, it was consumed with opportunism and lacked the desire to summon the proletariat to a revolutionary act. Thanks to its uncertain practical position, it often earned the sympathy of the radicalizing intelligentsia. If it could not throw off the yoke of militarism from the peoples even in peacetime, then it was even less capable of doing so at the moment when the "great" slaughter originated. Resolute steps were needed when the united world bourgeoisie faced off against the International, but it could not unite behind a single action. The bankruptcy of the Second International's practical position showed how weak still were its organization and its will to carry out resolute actions when needed.

This historical lesson did not pass in vain. From the sea of blood and tears and from the moans of the maimed, the Third International will emerge as an international organization of the revolutionary proletariat and of action. When the first Zimmerwald Conference met, we welcomed its "manifesto" to the proletarians of Europe as an attempt to gather the forces of the future International.

From the very beginning of war, the organizational connection between individual parts of the international proletariat was severed. The proletariat could do no more than defend its socialist conquests from the bourgeoisie, which was united against it. Now it is emerging from the stage of organizational fragmentation into the stage of unification on the basis of revolutionary action. From now on, comrades, the convictions held by each one of us will be tested by the degree of our participation in socialist organizations. From this moment, whoever is not with us is against us.

Get to work, comrades! *Go into the illegal social democratic workers' organizations!* Create your own student organizations for struggle against war and its perpetrators! Connect these organizations with the Russian Social Democratic Workers' Party. You should also work in legal democratic organizations in the spirit of fortifying socialist and revolutionary propaganda in them! Assume the initiative to act and speak out! By all possible means, you should dispel the fragmentary illusions that people can be emancipated by means of the all-Russian despot's bayonets! To work! To work, comrades!

You heard: "To you working men and women, mothers and fathers, widows and orphans, wounded and crippled, and to all victims of war, we appeal, extending hands to one another across all borders, blood-drenched fields, ruins of cities, and mountains of corpses: *Proletarians of all countries, unite!*" These are the words of the first Zimmerwald Manifesto. Do you hear them? "Two years of world war. Two years of devastation. Two years of bloodied victims and rabid reaction. Who will bear responsibility for this? Who hides behind those who cast the burning torch into the barrel of powder? Who wanted war and prepared for it already long ago? *The ruling classes did!*"

Do you hear, comrades: "Having laid millions of people in the grave, having plunged into sorrow millions of families, having turned millions of families into widows and orphans, having heaped up debris upon ruins, and having destroyed irreplaceable objects of cultural value, *the war entered into a dead end.*" "*There were neither victors nor conquered.* More accurately, *all were defeated,* became weak through loss of blood, were ruined, and were exhausted. Such are the results of this horror-filled war. Thus, the ruling classes' fantasies about imperialist world dominion did not come true."

Do you hear, citizens? "*During peacetime,* the capitalist system deprives the worker of any joy in life. *During war,* it deprives him of everything, even life. *Enough murder! Enough suffering! And enough devastation!* Use all the means at your disposal to promote the quickest possible conclusion to human slaughter! Demand an immediate end to the war! Ravaged and ruined peoples—raise yourselves up to struggle! Act more boldly! Remember that you are the majority, and if you want, you can become *a strong force*. Let the governments see that hatred toward war and the desire for social redemption grow in all countries. Then the hour of peace among peoples will approach. Down with war!"

These are the words of the second Zimmerwald manifesto: "To the ravaged and ruined peoples." This is the inviting voice of socialism! We are at the threshold of great events. They do not wait. Don't tarry, comrades! Take care not to arrive too late! Already the vanguard of the International has entered the blood-filled arena to halt the slaughter, to destroy the hateful slavery, and to create new forms of life. All new and large forces go forward to the victory of the revolution and toward the people's festival of insurrection. We will not stab them in the back. We will follow along behind them. So go ahead, comrades! Keep pace with workers in the ranks of the Russian Social Democratic Workers' Party under the proud, red banners of irreconcilable struggle!

Call the tsarist monarchy to account! Down with war! Long live the revolution! Forward! For the Provisional Revolutionary Government! For the Russian Democratic Republic! For socialism! Long live the Third International of the Revolutionary Proletariat!

Russian Social Democratic Workers' Party
December 1916[53]

"The Day of the People's Wrath Is Near"
January 9, 1917

On January 9, 1917, an estimated 150,000 workers in Petrograd (St. Peters-burg) carried out a protest strike against the war and the tsarist autocracy, a foreshock of the Russian Revolution that broke out six weeks later.

Historian Alexander Rabinowitch assessed the January 9 action so: "Elaborate plans for suppressing any major outbreaks were drawn up [by the government], and machine guns were positioned at strategic locations throughout the city. In an impressive display of working class solidarity more than 150,000 Petrograd workers went out on strike on January 9, the anniversary of Bloody Sunday. Some of the factories shut down that day were struck for the first time since 1905, and, equally significant, soldiers watching demonstrating workers were observed tipping their hats and cheering as red banners bearing revolutionary slogans were carried by."[54]

The following call for this action was circulated during the previous days by the Social Democratic Interdistrict Committee (Mezhraionka). January 9 was the anniversary of Bloody Sunday in 1905, when the tsarist government used military force to violently suppress a peaceful demonstration.

The Mezhraionka members wanted to rally all Marxist Social Demo-crats to unite the factions of the RSDRP, in order to present a united socialist front against the war, the autocracy, and liberal attempts to draw workers into a patriotic effort to support the war. The Mezhraionka was the current of the RSDRP that Leon Trotsky joined when he returned to Russia after the February Revolution in 1917. It fused with the Bolshevik current later in the year.[55]

For comparison, a translation of a leaflet issued by Petrograd Menshe-viks follows the Mezhraionka document.

* * *

Proletarians of all countries, unite!

Comrade workers! For the third time already, the anniversary of January 9, a day of great mourning, comes in the midst of a monstrous war, organized by the bourgeoisie and the nobles' government. War continues in its third year. The government sends millions of working people to the fronts to die without glory on distant battlefields and in filthy trenches. They die from hunger and cold or in bloody engagement with their toiling brothers, who are as completely innocent as are they.

What is the cause for which workers of all countries brutally slaughter, blow up, and murder one another in endless battles? What are the goals for which half of the European male population is maimed, crippled, and destroyed? The newspaper hacks, lackeys of the bourgeoisie, answer us in a harmonious chorus that war is waged for law and justice and for brotherhood and equality of all peoples. For these goals, according to them, millions of people slaughter and torture one another and innocent human blood flows.

Comrades! They want to conceal the truth with a lie. It is simply appalling that false, traitorous words about law, morality, and justice have served throughout to conceal the murder of millions. Our "lords," the nobles, bankers, and manufacturers, have always relied on lies while committing the vilest crimes. Their strength lies in deceit. Our ruling classes build their strength and their wealth on the ignorance and disunity of the people.

Only because of ignorance did our very brothers, dressed in military uniforms and cowed by military discipline, shoot at the insurrectionary proletariat and spill the blood of their defenseless fathers and mothers on the ill-omened square before the Winter Palace on January 9, 1905. With bayonets, whips, and bullets, the government suppressed the first Russian revolution in 1905 and 1906. "Don't be stingy with cartridges," ordered [Dmitry] Trepov.[56] But whose bayonets and bullets wounded and killed our comrades? They were the bayonets and bullets of workers and peasants who lacked consciousness.

It was cheap for the government and the bourgeoisie to achieve victory over the great revolution of 1905. Only several thousand workers perished and several hundred soldiers were killed. These

soldiers also were workers and peasants. Comrades, the entire autocratic government stays in power by keeping us split and by keeping
the working class unorganized. But we've accumulated twelve years
of experience. The bourgeoisie will not deceive us now! We will
remember without fail that our close relatives and dear friends die on
the front and their mothers and wives cry in the rear not for law and
justice, but so that "the fatherland's industry will prosper," as they
say in the ravings of the bourgeois newspapers.

Comrade soldiers! The bourgeoisie needs you to die to increase
its profits. It needs you to die so that there will be more room for
its cannibalism to expand! Russia is too small for them. Give them
Constantinople, the Bosporus, and the Dardanelles. Such greedy appetites guide the bourgeoisie of all combatant countries. Now there
are no defenders. Now they are all aggressors.

To weaken the resistance of the working class, the bourgeoisie
of each country calls on it to be patriotic and to defend the fatherland. Indeed, we do defend the fatherland, but not from an external
enemy. We defend it from an internal enemy, which is the tsarist
autocracy. We defend it from a gang of bandits, who started a war.
They are a band of murderers, who try to break the rebellious ranks
of the proletariat with calls for patriotism. The goal of the bourgeoisie and its newspaper servants is to send the proletariat in the wrong
direction.

There are traitors from our midst, the members of workers'
groups of the war industry committees, who forgot our class self-
consciousness, when they called for unification with the bourgeoisie. Gradually but definitively, they lost their proletarian convictions.
Lagging behind the bourgeoisie, they obediently repeat everything
that profits it. To them we say, "Hands off!"

At the beginning of the war, they spoke about civil peace.

Now the worker delegation under the Central War Industry
Committee falsifies the voice of the working class. It calls upon the
proletariat to carry out "mass political actions" to help the bourgeoisie in its war of words with the government. But they forgot that
the bourgeoisie, with Prince [Georgy] Lvov and [Pavel] Milyukov at
its head, struggles not against the entire police regime but against

individuals who are unable to organize a victorious war of conquest to secure Constantinople and the Straits for them. They forgot that the Milyukovs united with the Guchkovs to struggle against revolution and to renew the shattered trust in the bloody monarch.[57]

No, comrades, we and they do not follow the same path. Any help we might give to the bourgeoisie in its squabble with the government only makes it easier for it to achieve its goals of conquest, which postpones the revolution and has a disastrous impact upon our own situation.

Only we, the workers, the peasantry, and the long-suffering army are strong; we can only depend upon ourselves. So, comrades, let's go forward bravely along the path of the proletariat's class struggle. Let's remember that our proletarian tasks are still not resolved. Those demands, which were inscribed upon our banners of January 9, 1905, are still alive. We will struggle for socialism and a new life together and not just once, but in mighty association with the entire international proletariat, which is a worldwide, harmonious family.

Right now, our task is to create a powerful party organization. We Bolshevik and Menshevik Social Democrats call upon you comrades to create a single Social Democratic Workers' Party, so that a powerful proletariat can raise the army to revolt. By setting the strength of the proletariat and army against the nobility and the bureaucracy, the whole rotten police regime can be overthrown. On its ruins, a democratic republic can be created. Comrades, the day of the people's wrath is near. This will be a day of revenge and a day for trial and punishment of the debauched government, which has committed violence upon the popular masses.

Right now, we'll more resolutely close our ranks on January 9, the day of great sorrow and grief for the comrades whose lives were traitorously wasted in 1905. A steel chain of fraternal solidarity will more strongly bind us. Comrades, we'll shout harmoniously and powerfully: Revenge upon the aggressor who sits upon the throne. Ruin to tsarist stooges and murderers of the people, who use the blood and sweat of the people's labor to accumulate millions of fortunes for themselves. They feast during the plague time of the people's distress. By murdering husbands and sons, they force wives and mothers to pay the bills for their gain.

Comrades, we call upon you to commemorate those who fell in 1905 with a one-day strike on January 9. Forward, comrades! Arrange meetings and assemblies of protest against the war. Collect money for the victims of political repression and to fund the illegal press. On this day, the forces of the organized proletariat will pass under review. On this day, we should once more powerfully and unanimously shout:

Down with autocracy! Long live the revolution! Long live the Provisional Revolutionary Government! Down with war! Long live the Democratic Republic! Long live the international solidarity of the proletariat! Long live a united Russian Social Democratic Workers' Party!

Petersburg Interdistrict Committee [Mezhraionka]
January 1917[58]

★ ★ ★

Russian Social Democratic Workers' Party[59]
Proletarians of all countries, unite!

Comrades!

Twelve years ago, the streets of Petersburg overflowed with blood. The 300,000-member proletarian army was exposed to gunfire.

This was on January 9th.

Every year since then, on this day the working class of Russia exits the mills and factories. In memory of the sorrowful day of January 9, the working class celebrates its first mass demonstration of social-political struggle.

Calling upon the workers of Petersburg in this year to mark this memorial day with a strike, we organized Social Democratic Mensheviks propose to link this mass political demonstration with the greatest events of the present day. We propose to transform our annual day of mourning into the first energetic public demonstration in the struggle for peace.

Enough wasted blood! Enough tears!

Contrary to the will and desire of the ruling cliques who have forcibly drawn the peoples into fratricidal war, the moment has come for us to fraternally extend our hands to proletarians of all countries and openly declare:

We don't want war!

Long live peace!

We don't want the government and bourgeoisie, who profit from the coerced silence of the oppressed people, to insolently substitute their own opinion for ours.

We will not permit our fates to be decided without our involvement, for we think that the people themselves should decide their own fate.

Only the clearly expressed will of the proletarians of all countries can end the current carnage and achieve the peace desired by peoples of Europe.

This will not be the peace concluded by [Baron Boris] Stürmer[60] or his supporters, but a peace achieved by the will of the people. This will save the people of all countries at war from death and collapse.

The obsolete and hated monarchist political regime stands as an obstacle on the road to achieving that peace which the people desire. Therefore, when proclaiming the slogan of struggle for peace and reviewing our forces on the day of January 9, we should remember that peace of such a type is unthinkable without struggle against that which is old and outmoded.

We Russian workers are mobilizing our forces for struggle against the old regime and we are actively demonstrating for the peace desired by the international proletariat. Thus, we are preparing the ground for a joint, united demonstration for peace by proletarians of all countries.

Let our brothers on the other side of the trenches know that we expect from them such an activist demonstration for peace. Let's call out for convocation of an international worker congress, in which representatives of all countries should participate.

Down with war. Long live peace.

Down with the autocratic regime. Down with monarchy. Long live democracy. Long live the democratic republic.

Long live struggle for convocation of a popular constituent assembly.

Long live international solidarity of workers.

Long live the struggle for socialism.

Petersburg Initiative Group of Social Democratic Mensheviks[61]

LEAFLET 3

"Only a Provisional Government Can Bring Peace"

January 24, 1917

On January 24, 1917, a Menshevik-influenced workers' group within the Central War Industry Committee issued this appeal for a demonstration calling for a provisional government. The War Industry Committees were set up by businessmen in 1915 to assist the Russian imperial government with military supplies. Managers and engineers filled the committees, which were supplemented by groups of workers elected from factories. Bolsheviks and Socialist Revolutionaries were generally opposed to such collaboration by workers with owners and managers of industry, but some Mensheviks participated in the worker groups.

In early 1917, the Menshevik-composed Central Worker Group under the Central War Industry Committee attempted to mobilize workers to call for replacing the tsarist regime with a Provisional Government. The following appeal, with the full title "Only a Provisional Government Can Bring Freedom and Peace," led to the arrest of the members of the Central Worker Group beginning January 26, two days after the appeal's publication. The government postponed the convocation of the Duma until February 14; workers responded with a one-day strike rather than the mass demonstration suggested below.

This leaflet presents the views of the Menshevik current among Russian socialists, which would play the more moderate role throughout the Russian Revolution. The leaflet that follows this one is the reply of the other major current, the Bolsheviks.

★ ★ ★

The despotic regime is strangling the country. The autocracy's policy is worsening the already severe disasters of the war, which bear down with all their weight upon the classes which do not own property. And the government's self-seeking multiplies many times over the already countless victims of war.

The government, which created a severe crisis of food supply, is stubbornly pushing the country, day by day, toward hunger and complete ruin. It is using wartime circumstances to enserf the working class. By chaining the workers to the factory, it turns them into factory serfs. Incapable of coping with the tasks set by the war, the ruling regime nevertheless used it to intensify the persecution and oppression of Russia's various peoples.

Neither the war's end, nor the peace that the weary country thirsts for, can lead the people out of calamity, *if the war is ended by the current autocratic power rather than by the people themselves.*

Once they end the war, the autocracy will attempt to forge new chains for the people. Instead of relief, the end of the war can bring new, even more terrible misfortunes to the people. Bound hand and foot by the lack of political rights, the people, especially the proletariat, will be given over to arbitrariness, unemployment, and hunger. High prices and unemployment, together with the government's despotism, will cast the working class into poverty and slavery.

The working class and democratic forces can wait no longer. Each missed day is dangerous. The task now urgently posed for resolution is to decisively eliminate the autocratic regime and fully democratize the country. This is a matter of life and death for the working class and democratic forces.

Proceeding from everything stated above, the current conflict between propertied bourgeois society and the authorities clearly creates conditions especially favorable for the working class's active intervention. The people's movement can use the Duma's conflict with the government to promote a decisive blow against the autocracy.

We, the workers of _____, resolve: to immediately set about unifying and organizing our forces and electing a factory committee; to reach an understanding with comrades of other mills and factories; to explain to all comrades at many assemblies the extreme importance of this moment; and to provide information about our decisions to other factories.

We should be ready for a general, organized public initiative at the moment when the Duma (parliament) convenes.

Before the Duma convenes, let all of worker Petrograd, factory by factory, district by district, simultaneously move toward the Tauride Palace [the seat of the Duma], in order to present the main demands of the working class and democratic forces.

The entire country and the army should hear the voice of the working class. Only a Provisional Government, leaning for support on the people who have organized through struggle, can extricate the country from a dead end and fatal ruin, of strengthening political freedom within it, and of bringing about peace on conditions acceptable to both the Russian proletariat and the proletariat of other countries.[62]

LEAFLET 4

"For a Provisional Revolutionary Government of Workers and Poor Peasants"

February 1917

In February 1917, the Bolshevik Petersburg Committee of the Russian Social Democratic Workers' Party issued the following proclamation as a response to Menshevik appeals to workers to come out in support of the Duma (parliament) on the day of its convocation.

The Bolshevik committee warned workers not to trust attempts to ally them with Duma liberals, calling instead for a one-day strike on February 10, 1917, to commemorate the second anniversary of the trial of the Bolshevik deputies to the State Duma. The Petersburg Committee had forgotten, however, that many factories would be closed on that date, because it fell during a Russian religious holiday.

The Russian Bureau of the Bolshevik Central Committee, led by Alexander Shlyapnikov, urged the Petersburg Committee to transfer the date of the strike to February 13 and to consider extending the action to disrupt and take control of the initiative planned by the Worker Group of the Central War Industry Committee for February 14. The Petersburg Committee, however, proceeded with its original plan, which failed, due to the holiday. Nor did any workers respond to the Russian Bureau's call for a February 13 strike. The February Revolution would begin around International Women's Day on February 23.

* * *

Comrades!

The ruling classes have tightened the noose which they hung around the neck of the peoples of Europe. Millions of human lives have perished. The best and healthiest young forces of the people have been maimed or killed. Millions more suffer in captivity. Work comes to a halt, and there is hunger.

As many as fifteen million people from all combatant countries have lost their lives during the two years of slaughter, which have increased the profits of those with power in this world. What an unprecedented crime! Shame on those who undertook this mass extermination of the finest forces of the people! We, the worker vanguard and oppressed democratic forces, who spill our blood for a cause alien to us, face a great and difficult duty—to put an end to this crime!

And What Do They Do?

During the past two and a half years, have we heard even a weak voice of reason from the ruling classes, who dispose over the fate of the peoples whom they oppress? Now is the second anniversary of the trial of the representatives of the Russian working class in the State Duma. Since the very beginning of the war, the State Duma has cried out at its sessions for Russia's economy to flourish. Yet behind the walls of the Tauride Palace, the Duma ruins the economy by putting it at the mercy of the wolfish appetites of gentry landowners, capitalist factory owners, and bankers.

After our deputies were expelled from the State Duma, quickly tried and banished to remote, cold Siberia, the gentry landowners and capitalists rubbed their hands in satisfaction that they might speak more freely in the State Duma. But for two years, the State Duma has said nothing regarding the violation of its rights. It will also be silent on the second anniversary of deputies' exile. On the other hand, it will shout out and its agents will hustle about to seek among the working class, which it has decapitated, a sympathetic response to the servile speeches of "comradely" deputies.

And they can find some chauvinist groups of workers, who have been blinded by the tempest of war and who will carry Duma liberals' lustful cravings into the workers' midst. The most capricious rumors about the State Duma's intentions are circulating among workers now, on the eve of the proposed convocation of the State Duma on February 14. It is easy to see that the State Duma is not prepared to do anything new. But Duma liberals once more are not averse to making menacing gestures while protected by a wall of workers who have risen.

In the factories, workers heard the call to support the State Duma and even to push it to take a resolute step by presenting demands at the doors of the Tauride Palace. This summons is not only useless but also traitorous. Going in supplication to the palaces of tsars and ruling classes will dearly cost the credulous people who hoped to receive something from the inhabitants of these palaces.

Liberals and liberal worker politicians, when they do not have sufficient gunpowder, gladly dress up in front of the people as resolute warriors for the people's cause. But they conceal their actual intentions. Comrades, they come running to offer assistance so that you would allow them to surrender the country more fully to further military plunder and to endlessly wage war "to the end." They do not speak about this directly to us, but it is their fondest dream.

Our Appeal

We know what the fine words of liberals mean when they shout their dissatisfaction with the current government, yet secretly apportion among themselves future ministerial seats. From their tongues slip resolute phrases about taking power or about a "provisional government," depending on the organized people for support, yet they say not a word about war. We fully understand that only the mighty blow of democracy will put a stop to the harassment of the people and to their ordeal.

We should tell them: "All our efforts are directed against you and the war that you started. We are against the tsarist monarchy that you love so much because the monarch's scepter conceals your appetites and your dark deeds. We are against the tsarist government. You say you want to struggle against it, but you are afraid of its defeat, because only the tsarist government allows you to toy with the people."

We are for a democratic republic, which will put power into the hands of the people. We are for a provisional revolutionary government of workers and poor peasants. It will be able to convene a National Constituent Assembly based on universal, equal, direct, and secret suffrage. We are against the chauvinist criminal greed of each nation's capitalists, who divide up the world and inflict deep wounds upon it. We are for the international solidarity of workers, which will bring peace and happiness to the people.

On February 10, the anniversary of the day when the tsarist court struck a blow against our deputies, we will send them our fraternal greeting, for they gave their utmost strength in struggle for our slogans. We demand the immediate return of our deputies, and we will mark this anniversary by holding a one-day strike. This will be a sign of our readiness to give our lives in struggle for the demands that our exiled deputies proclaimed openly.

Down with tsarist monarchy! War on war! Long live the Provisional Revolutionary Government! Long live the National Constituent Assembly! Long live the Democratic Republic! Long live International Socialism![63]

LEAFLET 5

"A Day to Prepare for Conquering the Enemy"

February 21, 1917

On or about February 21, 1917, the Petrograd Mezhraionka (or Interdistrict Committee) distributed a leaflet regarding International Women's Day (IWD), to be celebrated two days later on February 23, which was March 8 on the Gregorian calendar (see Notes about the Text). That day became the first day of the 1917 Russian Revolution, sparked by a strike of women textile workers. Although the origins of IWD were in the United States, German Social Democrat Clara Zetkin proposed in 1910 an annual international celebration of the holiday. IWD was first celebrated in March 1911 in Germany and several other European countries. Russia followed with a small demonstration in 1913, but IWD in Russia was overshadowed by May Day and the anniversary of the Bloody Sunday massacre that took place on January 9, 1905.[64]

In 1917, Russia's various socialist groups failed to unite behind common slogans for International Women's Day and therefore were unable to carry out a joint action. Without a printing press at the time, the Bolsheviks did not issue any leaflets for IWD. The Interdistrict Committee, authors of the leaflet below, wanted to rally all the factions of the RSDRP in a united front against the war, the autocracy, and liberal attempts to draw workers into a patriotic effort to support the war. Later in 1917, the Interdistrict Committee, which Leon Trotsky joined when he returned to Russia, fused with the Bolshevik current.

According to historian Tsuyoshi Hasegawa, the Interdistrict Committee intended the leaflet below to educate workers, rather than provoke rebellion. None of the male socialists expected that on this holiday, women workers would provide the catalyst for the February Revolution, which would topple the autocracy.

Food shortages had become a routine occurrence by March 1917. On the morning of February 23, a fuel shortage in Petrograd stopped bakeries from working. Women (or their children) who had stood in line for hours had no bread to buy. Anticipating the cries of their children hungry for food, women *workers reached the limit of their patience. Women textile workers went on strike and appealed to metalworkers to join them. Radical socialists quickly decided to add slogans against the autocracy and war to the calls for bread.*

In this way, unexpectedly and on a commemorative day that most radical leftists treated as of minor importance, the February Revolution began.[65]

★ ★ ★

Working women comrades!

For ten years, women of all countries have observed February 23 as Women Workers' Day, as women's "May First." American women were the first to mark this as the day to review the state of their forces. Gradually, women of the entire world joined them. On this day, meetings and assemblies are held at which attempts are made to explain the reasons for our difficult situation and to show the way out of it.

It has been a long time since women first entered the factories and mills to earn their bread. For a long time, millions of women have stood at the machines all day on an equal footing with men. Factory owners work both male and female comrades to exhaustion. Both men and women are thrown in jail for going on strike. Both men and women need to struggle against the owners. But women entered the family of workers later than men. Often, they still are afraid and do not know what they should demand or how to demand it. The owners have always used their ignorance and timidity against them and still do.

On this day, especially, comrades, let's think about how we can conquer our enemy, the capitalist, as quickly as possible. We will remember our near and dear ones on the front. We will recall the difficult struggle they waged to wring from the owners each extra ruble of pay and each hour of rest, and each liberty from the government. How many of them fell at the front, or were cast into prison or exile for their brave struggle? You replaced them in the rear, in the mills and factories. Your duty is to continue their great cause—that of emancipating all humanity from oppression and slavery.

Women workers, you should not hold back those male comrades who remain, but rather you should join them in fraternal struggle against the government and the factory owners. It is for their sake that war is waged, so many tears are shed, and so much blood is spilled in all countries. This terrible slaughter has now gone into its third year. Our fathers, husbands, and brothers are perishing. Our dear ones arrive home as unfortunate wretches and cripples. The tsarist government sent them to the front. It maimed and killed them, but it does not care about their sustenance.

There is no end in sight to the shedding of workers' blood. Workers were shot down on Bloody Sunday, January 9, 1905, and massacred during the Lena Goldfields strike in April 1912. More recently, workers were shot in Ivanovo-Voznesensk, Shuya, Gorlovka, and Kostroma. Workers' blood is shed on all fronts. The empress trades in the people's blood and sells off Russia piece by piece. They send nearly unarmed soldiers to certain death by shooting. They kill hundreds of thousands of people on the front and they profit financially from this.

Under the pretext of war, owners of factories and mills try to turn workers into serfs. The cost of living grows terribly high in all cities. Hunger knocks at everyone's door. From the villages, they take away cattle and the last morsels of bread for the war. For hours, we stand in line for food. Our children are starving. How many of them have been neglected and lost their parents? They run wild and many become hooligans. Hunger has driven many girls, who are still children, to walk the streets. Many children stand at machines doing work beyond their physical capacity until late at night. Grief and tears are all around us.

It is hard for working people not only in Russia, but in all countries. Not long ago, the German government cruelly suppressed an uprising of the hungry in Berlin. In France, the police are in a fury. They send people to the front for going on strike. Everywhere, the war brings disaster, a high cost of living, and oppression of the working class.

Comrades, working women, for whose sake is war waged? Do we need to kill millions of Austrian and German workers and peasants? German workers did not want to fight either. Our close ones do not go willingly to the front. They are forced to go. The

Austrian, English, and German workers go just as unwillingly. Tears accompany them in their countries as in ours.

War is waged for the sake of gold, which glitters in the eyes of capitalists, who profit from it. Ministers, mill owners, and bankers hope to fish in troubled waters. They become rich in wartime. After the war, they will not pay military taxes. Workers and peasants will bear all the sacrifices and pay all the costs.

Dear women comrades, will we keep on tolerating this silently for very long, with occasional outbursts of boiling rage against small-time traders? Indeed, it is not they who are at fault for the people's calamities. They are ruined themselves. The government is guilty. It began this war and cannot end it. It ravages the country. It is its fault that you are starving. The capitalists are guilty. It is waged for their profit. It's well-nigh time to shout to them: Enough! Down with the criminal government and its entire gang of thieves and murderers. Long live peace!

Already the day of retribution approaches. A long time ago, we ceased to believe the tales of the government ministers and the masters. Popular rage is increasing in all countries. Workers everywhere are beginning to understand that they can't expect their governments to end the war. If they do conclude peace, it will entail attempts to take others' land, to rob another country, and this will lead to new slaughter. Workers do not need that which belongs to someone else.

Down with the autocracy! Long live the Revolution! Long live the Provisional Revolutionary Government! Down with war! Long live the Democratic Republic! Long live the international solidarity of the proletariat! Long live the united RSDRP!

Petersburg Interdistrict Committee[66]

LEAFLET 6
"For a General Strike against Autocracy"
February 27, 1917

On February 27, 1917, socialists in Petrograd distributed the following appeal for an insurrectionary general strike to bring down tsarism. That day, in the culmination of Russia's February revolution, tsarist power crumbled with the fall of Nicholas II.

The day after the demonstration by women workers on February 23, more than two hundred thousand striking workers marched into the center of Petrograd. Large numbers of students and middle-class professionals joined the demonstrations on February 25. Soldiers at first hesitated to forcefully remove demonstrators, but on February 26, some soldiers followed orders to shoot at demonstrators, killing hundreds.

As the senior member of the Russian Bureau of the Bolshevik Central Committee in Petrograd, Alexander Shlyapnikov encouraged workers to win soldiers over to their side during the first days of the February Revolution, but felt that armed struggle by socialists against the government was premature. Preferring direct armed action, the Bolshevik Vyborg District Committee scorned Shlyapnikov's position as denying the revolutionary character of the ongoing demonstrations.

The Petersburg Committee of the RSDRP called for Bolsheviks to take practical measures to organize and accelerate the pace of revolutionary developments. Yet the Interdistrict Committee (Mezhraionka) of the RSDRP may have had the most influence upon radical socialist workers and soldiers during the February Revolution. It encouraged workers to prolong their strike and called upon soldiers to defend workers against police attacks.

The mutiny of the Volynsky regiment on February 27 set an example for other soldiers. The February Revolution culminated that day, as Duma liberals formed a committee that would become the nucleus of the Provisional Government, tsarist ministers resigned, and socialists formed the Petrograd Soviet of Workers' and Soldiers' Deputies.[67]

* * *

Proletarians of all countries, unite!

Comrade workers! They are shooting us down! Workers' blood has been spilled on the streets of Petrograd! Hungry people rose to struggle, but the tsar made them eat lead. Just as on January 9, 1905, when the servants of the autocracy shot down workers who went to the tsar for justice and mercy, on February 25–26 they shot down hungry workers who went onto the streets to protest hunger and the reigning arbitrariness.

Comrades! They have committed a terrible, senseless, monstrous crime. During these days of the people's rage and of merciless retribution against them, we were helpless against the policemen and handfuls of soldiers who were loyal to the tsar. We could not fight back against their blows or take a life for a life. We were unarmed. Our fists were clenched in impotent rage. They beat us with their swords, their horses trampled us, and the defenseless people fled with hatred in their hearts toward the enemy.

Comrades! During these difficult days, the working class saw more clearly than ever before that without strong, powerful, proletarian organizations, fighting detachments, and without the army's support for the people, we won't break the enemy and destroy autocracy. Likewise, we learned during these days that our brothers the soldiers do not always obey orders to carry out fratricide. We hail the Cossacks who chased the mounted police from Znamenskaya Square. We hail and give fraternal thanks to the soldiers of the Pavlovsky Regiment who shot at a detachment of mounted police near the Cathedral of Resurrection.

Soldiers are beginning to see the light. They understand that their enemy is not the starving, oppressed people, but the tsarist autocracy. During these difficult days for workers, only part of the soldiers, students, and citizens supported us. The State Duma, which is not truly representative of the people, is criminally silent. While the stones cry out for vengeance, the State Duma is deaf and blind to the people's woe.

Comrades! Not only do they shoot us down, but they also cast us onto the streets to suffer hunger and destitution. Putilov and

Trubochny factories have been shut down. Fifty thousand workers have been deprived of a morsel of bread!

Comrades! Whoever still has a conscience and is neither a slave nor a pitiful traitor to the workers' cause will hear our appeal and will join us to unanimously protest merciless international war.

Comrades! Bring activity in the city to a standstill. Let all the factories, mills, workshops, and printing presses come to a halt. Let the electricity go out. We summon you to a general strike of protest, to strike a blow against the despotic autocracy. We, the Social Democratic Bolsheviks and Mensheviks and the Socialist Revolutionaries, summon the proletariat of Petersburg and of all Russia to organize and feverishly mobilize our forces.

Comrades! Organize underground strike committees in the mills and factories and link districts to one another. Collect funds for underground printing presses and for weapons. Get ready, comrades! The hour of decisive struggle approaches. We will not fear General [Sergey] Khabalov [Petrograd military district commander], who dares to call us traitors. It is not we workers who betray the people, but those traitors and murderers, the [Vladimir] Sukhomlinovs [war minister] and the Khabalovs. The State Duma and the liberals betray the people.

Comrades! Khabalov orders us to go back to work on the 28th, but we summon you to struggle and to a general strike!

Be brave! All for one and one for all!

Long live the general political strike of protest!

Always remember our fallen brothers!

Down with war!

Down with autocracy!

Long live revolution!

Long live the Provisional Revolutionary Government!

Long live the Constituent Assembly!

Long live a democratic republic!

Long live the international solidarity of the proletariat!

Petersburg Interdistrict Committee of the RSDRP[68]

LEAFLET 7

"Soldiers, Take Power into Your Own Hands!"

March 1, 1917

On March 1, 1917, the Social Democratic Interdistrict Committee (Mezhraionka), supported by the Petersburg Committee of Socialist Revolutionaries, issued an appeal to soldiers. At that time, the Duma Committee and the Petrograd Soviet of Workers' and Soldiers' Deputies were striving to bring order to the revolutionary events on the streets and to prevent the tsarist autocracy from restoring its control over the city. Dominated by moderate socialists, the Soviet pursued a policy of cooperation with liberals in the Duma. Nonetheless, the Soviet's "Order No. 1," issued on March 1 in response to soldiers' pressure and published on March 2, called for soldiers to elect representative committees all along the chain of command, stipulated that officers treat soldiers respectfully, and asserted the Soviet's primary influence over soldiers by stating that they should obey only Duma commands that did not contradict soviet resolutions.

The Duma Committee announced the formation of the Provisional Government on March 2, and Nicholas II abdicated on behalf of himself and his son. By March 3, the autocracy had collapsed. Thus, the ground had been prepared for the period of "dual power" in Petrograd—between the rival Duma and Provisional Government and the Petrograd Soviet—that prevailed between the February and October Revolutions.

The Interdistrict Committee, coauthors of the appeal below, wanted to rally all the factions of the RSDRP, but later in 1917 fused with the Bolshevik current. Their leaflet here presented a militant alternative to the Duma Committee's course. According to historian Michael Melancon, it circulated on March 1, 1917, probably before Order No. 1 was issued, and may have influenced the wording of Order No. 1. Alexander Shlyapnikov, who published the leaflet in 1923, states that the Executive Committee of the Petrograd Soviet confiscated it on the morning of March 2.[69]

* * *

Comrade soldiers!

It has come to pass! You enslaved peasants and workers arose, and with a crash the autocratic government collapsed in disgrace.

Soldiers! The people were patient for a long time. The peasants long suffered under the power of the gentry landowners, the land captains, the district police officers, and the whole gang of servants of the tsarist autocracy. Millions of peasants became swollen from hunger while the State Treasury, the monasteries, and the landowners seized all the land, and while the nobles got fat from sucking the people's blood. Without land, the peasant cannot even put his chickens out to feed!

Brother soldiers!

As peasants, as workers, what do you need? All the land and full freedom—that is what you need! You did not shed your blood in vain. For two days Petrograd has been under the power of soldiers and workers. It has been two days since the dissolved State Duma elected a Provisional Committee, which it calls a Provisional Government. Still, you have not heard a word from [Mikhail] Rodzyanko [chair of the Duma] or [Pavel] Milyukov [Kadet Party leader and Provisional Committee spokesman] about whether the land will be taken from the gentry landowners and given to the people. The prospects are poor!

Soldiers! Be on your guard to prevent the nobles from deceiving the people!

Go ask the Duma: Will the people have land, freedom, and peace?

Soldiers! Why does the Duma say nothing about this? Autocratic arbitrariness needs to be completely uprooted. The people's cause will perish unless we conclude the business by convening the Constituent Assembly, to which *all* peasants and *all* workers would send their deputies—not like in the current Duma, composed of the wealthy and highest ranks of society, which dooms the people's cause!

Take power into your hands, so that this Romanov gang of nobles and officers does not deceive you. Elect your own platoon, company, and regiment commanders. Elect company committees for managing food supplies. All officers should be under the supervision of these company committees.

Accept only those officers whom you know to be friends of the people.

Obey only delegates sent from the Soviet of Workers' and Soldiers' Deputies!

Soldiers! Now, when you have arisen and achieved victory, those coming to join you include not only friends but also officers, who are former enemies and who only pretend to be your friends.

Soldiers! We are more afraid of the fox's tail [intrigues] than the wolf's tooth [outright aggression]. Only the workers and peasants are your true friends and brothers. Strengthen your unity with them! Send your delegate-representatives to the Soviet of Workers' and Soldiers' Deputies, already supported by 250,000 workers in Petrograd alone. Your representatives and worker deputies should become the people's Provisional Revolutionary Government. It will give you both land and freedom!

Soldiers, listen to us! Demand an answer from the Duma right now. Will it take land from the gentry landowners, state treasury, and monasteries? Will it transfer land to the peasants? Will it give the people complete freedom? Will it convene the Constituent Assembly? Don't waste time!

Soldiers! Talk about this in your companies and battalions! Hold meetings! Elect from among you commanders and representatives to the Soviet of Workers' and Soldiers' Deputies.

All land to the peasants!

All freedom to the people!

Long live the Soviet of Workers' and Soldiers' Deputies!

Long live the Provisional Revolutionary Government!

Petersburg Interdistrict Committee of the RSDRP
Petersburg Committee of Socialist Revolutionaries
March 1917[70]

LEAFLET 8

"Joining Together to Achieve Peace"

March 14, 1917

On March 14, the Petrograd Soviet issued the following appeal "To the Peoples of the World" calling for a restoration of workers' unity in the cause of peace.

The moderate socialists, known as the Mensheviks, who dominated the Petrograd Soviet until September 1917, pursued a policy of "revolutionary defensism," which advocated military defense of Russia and its revolution against what they perceived as German aggression while calling upon European socialists to pressure their governments to bring about peace.

This policy toward the war would not be consistently defined until the return of Irakli Tsereteli and other Menshevik leaders from Siberian exile on March 20. Therefore, the document below reflects the views in the Soviet at a time when moderate socialists were still open to making concessions to their radical counterparts regarding the Soviet's position on the war and other issues. Discussions in the Soviet were crucial to the realignment of leftist forces that occurred in the wake of the February Revolution.

The following leaflets will take up how the "revolutionary defensism" policy worked out in practice.[71]

* * *

Comrades, proletarians, and laborers of all countries!

We Russian workers and soldiers, united in the Petrograd Soviet of Workers' and Soldiers' Deputies, send you our heartfelt greetings while announcing a great event. Our Russian democracy has extinguished the centuries-old tsarist despotism. We now join your family as a member with full rights and as a formidable force in the struggle for our mutual emancipation. Ours is a great victory for worldwide freedom and democracy. The "policeman of Europe" and the chief buttress of world reaction is no more. Indeed, it has been buried never to rise again. Long live freedom! Long live the international solidarity of the proletariat and its struggle for final victory!

Our cause has still not fully triumphed. The vestiges of the old order have not yet dispersed. Enemies of the Russian Revolution are gathering their forces against it. Nevertheless, our gains are enormous. The peoples of Russia will express their will in the Constituent Assembly, which will be convened very soon based on universal, equal, direct, and secret suffrage. Already, we can predict with confidence that a democratic republic will triumph in Russia.

The Russian people possess full political freedom. They can now speak authoritatively about the country's domestic and foreign policy. Appealing to all the peoples who have been ruined and destroyed in this horrific war, we declare that the time has come to struggle resolutely against aggression by governments of all countries. The time has come for all peoples to resolve the question of war and peace.

Cognizant of its revolutionary strength, Russian democracy declares that it will oppose by all means the ruling classes' aggressive policy. It calls upon the peoples of Europe to speak and act out jointly and resolutely to foster peace.

We appeal to our brothers, the proletarians of the Austro-German coalition, and above all to the German proletariat. From the very beginning of the war, we were convinced that by taking up arms against Russian autocracy you were defending European culture from Asian despotism. Many of you believed that this justified your support for the war. Now this justification no longer exists. Democratic Russia cannot threaten freedom and civilization.

We will firmly defend our own freedom from any kind of reactionary encroachments, whether internal or external. The Russian Revolution will not retreat from the bayonets of the conquerors and will not be crushed by foreign military force. We call upon you to throw off the yoke of your semi-autocratic order just as the Russian people shook off tsarist despotism. You should refuse to serve as a weapon of invasion and violence in the hands of kings, gentry landowners, and bankers. Together in friendship we will put a stop to the terrible slaughter, which disgraces humankind and casts a shadow over the great days of the birth of Russian freedom.

Working people of all countries! Across mountains of our brothers' corpses, across rivers of innocent blood and tears, across smoking ruins of towns and villages, and across lost cultural treasures, we extend to you a fraternal hand and summon you to a renewed and strengthened international unity. This will secure our future victories and the full emancipation of humanity.

Proletarians of all countries, unite!

Petrograd Soviet of Workers' and Soldiers' Deputies[72]

LEAFLETS 9 AND 10
Calling for Peace . . . and Renewed Offensives

On May 2, the Executive Committee of the Petrograd Soviet of Workers' and Soldiers' Deputies issued two appeals—one to socialists of all countries calling "for an international socialist conference" to demand an end to the First World War; and the other to Russian soldiers at the front calling for "military strength" to "[serve] the cause of peace." At this point in 1917, the leadership of the Petrograd Soviet was composed of more moderate socialists—the left-wing and adamantly antiwar Bolsheviks were a minority for now.

In the days leading up to the appeals, liberal figures in the Provisional Government had talked with moderate socialist leaders of the Soviet about forming a centrist and more broadly representative government. Radical socialists opposed this effort. Nevertheless, with moderates holding a majority in the Soviet, some of the socialists consented on May 1 to join the Provisional Government to prevent a looming political crisis. The new government, comprising six socialists and ten non-socialists, was announced on May 5.

Despite being called a "coalition," the new government did not function harmoniously, for significant differences remained between socialists and liberals over social and economic reform. The May 2 appeals from the Soviet reflect the new relationship between it and the Provisional Government.[73]

Russian revolutionary Alexander Shlyapnikov wrote in his memoirs that these calls contained "empty phrases" aimed less at stirring revolutionary sentiment abroad than at stifling it within Russia. The appeal to soldiers sharply condemned their spreading initiatives to fraternize with "enemy" soldiers on the other side of the front line. Shlyapnikov summed it up as an appeal to "struggle for peace—and a military offensive." The leaflets translated below show how left-wing socialists challenged both the new political alignment in the Provisional Government and the politics expressed by the Soviet executive of early May.

LEAFLET 9

"To Socialists Abroad: 'For an International Socialist Conference'"

May 2, 1917

To Socialists of all countries: Comrades!

The Russian Revolution was born in the flames of world war. This war is a monstrous crime committed by imperialists of all countries. Their greed for conquest and their insane arms race prepare for worldwide conflagration and make it inevitable.

No matter who will win militarily, the imperialists of all countries share victory in this war, which has monstrously profited them. They are amassing colossal capital in their hands, which is the reason for their unprecedented power over individual lives and labor.

But for the exact same reason, laborers of all countries are this war's losers. Countless victims are sacrificed on the altar of imperialism, where they lose their lives, their health, their fortune, and their freedom. They carry the burden of unspeakable deprivations.

The Russian Revolution, which is a revolution of laboring people—workers and soldiers—is an uprising not only against tsarism, but also against the horrors of worldwide slaughter. This is the first indignant cry by a detachment of the international army of labor against the crimes of international imperialism. This is not only national revolution, but also the first stage of international revolution, which will end the disgrace of war and return peace to humanity.

From the very moment of its birth, the Russian Revolution distinctly recognized the international task confronting it. Its authoritative body—the Petrograd Soviet of Workers' and Soldiers' Deputies—in its appeal of March 14 summoned all peoples of the world to unite in the struggle for peace.

The revolutionary democratic forces of Russia do not want a separate peace, which would free the hands of the Austro-German alliance. They know that a separate peace would betray the cause of worker democracy in all countries. The forces of worker democracy would be bound hand and foot before the world of victorious imperialism. They know that a separate peace could lead to the military defeat of other countries. This result would for many years fortify the victory of chauvinism and revenge in Europe, which would remain an armed camp, as it was after the Franco-Prussian War of 1870. A new bloody fight would soon become inevitable.

Russia's revolutionary democratic forces want universal peace on conditions acceptable to laborers of all countries. They do not strive for annexations or plunder. Instead, they want all peoples to freely express their will and they want to reduce the power of international imperialism. Lacking ulterior motives and acting with proletarian intellect and emotion, they have adopted the formula of peace without annexations and indemnities based on the self-determination of peoples. It provides the central platform on which laborers of all countries, both combatant and neutral, can come together to establish enduring peace and to heal the wounds dealt by bloody war.

The Provisional Government of revolutionary Russia adopted this platform, and the revolutionary democratic forces of Russia appeal first to you, the socialists of Allied powers. You should not allow the voice of the Russian Provisional Government to remain alone among the Allied powers. You should force your governments to declare decisively and definitively that they share the platform of peace without annexations and indemnities, based on self-determination of peoples. In this way, you will attach proper gravity and force to the act of the Russian government.

You will give confidence to our revolutionary army, which carries on its banners the slogan "Peace among peoples," that its wounded and fallen will not be used for evil purposes. You will make it possible for it to fulfill its entire allotted share of fighting tasks with all of its revolutionary enthusiasm. You will strengthen its faith that by defending revolutionary advances and our freedom, it simultaneously struggles for the interests of all international democratic forces and makes the desired peace come more quickly. You will also confront the governments of warring countries with the need either to decisively and irrevocably reject the policy of conquest, plunder, and violence, or to openly recognize their crimes, and so rain down upon their heads the righteous anger of their peoples.

To you socialists of the Austro-German alliance, the revolutionary democratic forces of Russia appeal not to allow your governments' military forces to act as the executioners of Russian freedom. The revolutionary Russian army has been enveloped by a joyous mood of freedom and brotherhood. You must not permit your governments to transfer troops to the Western front to destroy France, then attack Russia, and finally suffocate you and the rest of the international proletariat in the global chokehold of imperialism.

The revolutionary democratic forces of Russia appeal to socialists of combatant and neutral countries to prevent the triumph of imperialism. Let the efforts of the international proletariat bring the campaign for peace, which the Russian Revolution began, to a successful conclusion.

To unify these efforts, the Petrograd Soviet of Workers and Soldiers' Deputies decided to assume the initiative to convene an international conference of all socialist parties and currents of all countries. No matter what disagreements have split socialism during three years of war, no current of the proletariat should refuse to participate in the joint struggle for peace, which has been put on the agenda of the Russian Revolution.

We are confident, comrades, that we will see representatives of all socialist groups at the conference we have convened.

The unanimous decision of the proletarian International will be the first victory of laborers over the international of imperialists.

Proletarians of all countries, unite![74]

LEAFLET 10

"Appeal to Soldiers: 'Military Strength Serves the Cause of Peace'"

May 2, 1917

Comrade soldiers at the front!

On behalf of the revolutionary democratic forces of Russia, we ardently appeal to you.

Yours is a difficult fate. By the dear price of your blood, you paid for the crimes of the tsar who sent you to fight and who left you without weapons, bullets, and bread. Indeed, the tsar and his stooges bear responsibility for the deprivations that you are now suffering, for they have allowed the country to rot and become exhausted. The revolution will require much more effort to overcome the devastation that it inherited from the robbers and butchers.

The laboring people did not need war and they did not start it. Rulers and capitalists of all countries brought it about. For the people, each day of war is an extra woe. Having toppled the tsar from the throne, the Russian people made its first task to end the war as quickly as possible.

The Soviet of Workers' and Soldiers' Deputies appealed to all peoples to end the war. It appealed to the French, the Germans, and the Austrians.

Russia awaits an answer to this appeal.

But remember, comrade soldiers, our appeal will not be worth anything, if [Kaiser] Wilhelm's regiments defeat revolutionary Russia before our brothers—the workers and peasants of other countries—respond.

Our appeal will be worthless unless it is supported by the entire power of the revolutionary people and if Wilhelm Hohenzollern secures his triumph over the ruins of Russian freedom. Free Russia's downfall will be an enormous, irreparable misfortune not only for us, but also for the laborers of the entire world. Comrade soldiers! Defend revolutionary Russia with all your strength!

Workers and peasants of Russia strive toward peace with all their heart. But it should be a universal peace for all peoples by their general agreement. What will happen if we want a separate peace only for ourselves? What will happen if the Russian armed forces drive their bayonets into the ground today and say that they do not want to fight any more, that what goes on in the rest of the world is none of their business?

What will happen is that German imperialism, having defeated our allies in the West, will fall upon us with all the strength of its weaponry. What will happen is that the German emperor, landowners, and capitalists will place their heavy heel upon our necks, will seize our towns, villages, and land, and will impose the yoke of tribute upon the Russian people.

Really, did we cast off the yoke of Nicholas, in order to bow down before Wilhelm?

Comrade soldiers! The Soviet of Workers' and Soldiers' Deputies leads you to peace along a different path. We lead you to peace by calling for an uprising, for a revolution by the workers and peasants of Germany and Austro-Hungary. We lead you to peace by winning from our government a rejection of the policy of aggression and by demanding the same rejection from the Allied powers.

We lead you to peace by convening an international congress of socialists of the entire world for a joint, decisive uprising against war. Comrade soldiers, it is time for the peoples of all countries to wake up. It is time for them to arise and with an iron hand force their kings and capitalists to move toward peace. It is time for laborers of all countries to close ranks with us in a merciless struggle against aggressors and robbers.

But you remember, comrade soldiers. This time will never arrive if you fail to hold back the enemy's onslaught at the front, if your ranks are crushed, and if the lifeless corpse of Russian Revolution lies at Wilhelm's feet.

Remember, comrades. You now stand guard for Russian freedom at the front in the trenches. You defend the Russian Revolution. You defend your brothers, the workers, and peasants. Let this defense be worthy of the great cause and of the great sacrifices already imposed on you! No matter what, you can't defend the front by sitting still in the trenches. The enemy's attack can only be prevented by going on the offensive.

To wait for attack one more time means to await death submissively. Only by going onto the offensive is it possible to save yourselves and your brothers on other sectors of the front from death and ruin.

Remember this, comrade soldiers. Having vowed to defend Russian freedom, don't reject the coming actions which military circumstances demand. Russia's freedom and fortune are in your hands.

Beware of traps and provocations while you are defending this freedom. The fraternization which is developing at the front can easily become a trap. With whom may revolutionary forces fraternize? They may fraternize with another revolutionary army, which has resolved to die for peace and freedom. But the German and Austrian armies are not yet revolutionary, no matter how many ideologically conscious and honest individuals are in them. They still have no revolution there. The military forces there still follow the emperors Wilhelm [of Germany] and Karl [of Austria-Hungary], the gentry landowners, and the capitalists. They support seizure of other people's land, plunder, and violence. Their military high command exploits not only your trust but also the blind obedience of its own soldiers.

You fraternize sincerely, yet you are met with an officer of the general staff who emerges from the enemy trenches disguised in a soldier's uniform.

You speak with the opponent without any cunning. Meanwhile, his commander photographs the terrain. You cease fire to fraternize, yet during this time the enemy moves artillery, constructs fortifications, and transfers forces behind its trenches.

Comrade soldiers! You will not achieve peace through fraternization, nor with tacit agreements concluded at the front by individual companies, battalions, and regiments. The salvation of the revolution and the triumph of peace across the world do not lie in a separate peace or in a separate truce. People who assure you that fraternization is the path to peace are leading you to your death and to the death of Russian freedom. Don't believe them.

There is a different road to peace. The Soviet of Workers' and Soldiers' Deputies pointed it out to you. Support it. Sweep away everything that weakens your military strength and that brings demoralization into the army. Your military strength serves the cause of peace. The Soviet of Workers' and Soldiers' Deputies can only struggle for revolution and peace if you prevent Russia's military rout.

Comrade soldiers! The workers and peasants not only of Russia, but of the entire world, put their trust and hope in you. Soldiers of the revolution, be worthy of this trust, knowing that your fighting serves the cause of peace.

Carry out your military duty with unwavering resolution, in the name of revolutionary Russia's happiness and freedom and the future brotherhood of peoples![75]

LEAFLETS 11 AND 12

A Bolshevik Appeal Finds an Echo in the Streets

On June 9, the Bolshevik Party circulated the first proclamation below, drafted by Joseph Stalin, with the aim of reaching workers in Petrograd. Nine days later, the Bolsheviks' slogans promoted in this appeal won mass support at a giant demonstration called by the Petrograd Soviet.

In mid-May, the Bolshevik Military Organization (BMO) had proposed to the party's Central Committee (CC) a demonstration opposing the Provisional Government's planned military offensive. Fearing that such an action was premature, the CC was not receptive. BMO organizers became more insistent over the coming weeks, as soldiers worried about attempts to restore military discipline and to transfer them to the front.

BMO leaders hoped to time a demonstration to coincide with the First All-Russian Congress of Soviets of Workers' and Soldiers' Deputies, which met in Petrograd June 3–24. The CC remained undecided—Lenin supported a demonstration, as did most Petrograd committee members, while Kamenev was against.

Worker unrest over the Provisional Government's attempt to expel anarchist-communists from its headquarters created more friction. An expanded meeting of Bolshevik Party organizations on June 8 revealed majority support for a demonstration by workers and soldiers on June 10. The Bolshevik leaflet helped prepare for the demonstration.

The second document is the response by the All-Russian Congress of Soviets to the Bolsheviks' appeal. The demonstration proposed by the Bolsheviks encountered opposition in the Congress, which appealed to military units and factory workers not to march. In the early morning hours of June 10, a small meeting of Bolshevik CC members called off the demonstration.

Attempting to bolster support for its policies, the Soviet arranged a demonstration on June 18, which attracted almost five hundred thousand participants. However, due to the efforts of Bolsheviks, Left SRs, and an-archists, this demonstration was dominated not by the moderate politics that still predominated in the soviets, but by radical slogans for ending the war, opposing the coalition government and its military offensive, and transferring all power to the soviets—precisely what the Bolsheviks had argued for.[76]

LEAFLET 11

"The Bolshevik Proclamation Calling for a Demonstration"

June 9, 1917

To all laborers, workers, and soldiers of Piter [Petrograd]: Comrades! Russia is experiencing difficult trials. The war, which has carried off millions of victims, continues. Millionaire bankers are intentionally prolonging it, because they're making a fortune off the war. The war has devastated industry, leading to factory stoppages and unemployment. The greedy capitalists, who lock out workers while making fantastic profits, exacerbate this trend.

Shortages of bread and other food supplies are becoming more acute. The increase in the cost of living is throttling the population. Prices keep increasing, per the whims of robber-speculators.

The sinister specter of hunger and ruin looms over us. At the same time, the black clouds of counterrevolution are approaching.

Imposed by the tsar to strangle the people, the [illegitimate] June 3rd Duma now demands an immediate offensive at the front. But for what purpose? To drown in blood the freedom that we have obtained.

The State Council, which supplied the tsar with hangmen ministers, is quietly braiding a traitor's noose, while shielding itself behind the law. What is this for? It is so that at a convenient time they may come out into the open and hang the noose around the neck of the people.

The Provisional Government, positioned between the tsarist Duma and the Soviet and containing ten bourgeois members, obviously has fallen under the influence of gentry landowners and capitalists. Instead of securing soldiers' rights, Kerensky's "declaration" violates their rights in several very important points.

Instead of securing the liberties that soldiers gained during the revolution, new "commands" threaten them with penal servitude.

Instead of securing the freedom that Russia's citizens achieved, there are arrests without trial or investigation, and new suggestions about Article 129, which make threats about penal servitude.

Instead of struggling against counterrevolution, they put up with the debauchery and bacchanalia of counterrevolutionaries.

Meanwhile, economic devastation is getting worse and no measures are taken against it.

The war keeps going on, and no actual measures are taken to end it.

Famine is still imminent, and no actual measures are taken to prevent it.

Is it really any surprise that counterrevolutionaries are becoming more insolent and inciting the government to repress soldiers, sailors, workers, and peasants?

Comrades! It's impossible to endure such things in silence any more. It is a crime to keep silent after all this! Protest is already beginning in the depths of the working class. We are free citizens. We have the right to protest and we should avail ourselves of this right before it is too late.

We still have the right to demonstrate peacefully. We will go to a peaceful demonstration and will make our needs and wishes known!

Raise the flags of victory today to make the enemies of freedom and socialism afraid!

Let our call, the cry of the sons of the revolution, fly round all Russia today to the joy of all those who are oppressed and enslaved!

Workers! Join together with soldiers and support their just demands. Indeed, don't you remember how they supported you during the revolution? Everyone onto the streets, comrades!

Soldiers! Hold out your hands to workers and support their just demands. The strength of the revolution is in the union of soldiers and workers. Not one regiment or company should sit in the barracks today!

Everyone into the streets, comrades! March on the streets of the capital in orderly ranks. State your wishes calmly and confidently, as befits the strong:

Down with the tsarist Duma!

Down with the State Council!

Down with the ten capitalist ministers!

All power to the All-Russian Soviet of Workers', Soldiers', and Peasants' Deputies!

Revise the "declaration of the rights of soldiers"!

Repeal the "commands" against soldiers and sailors!

Down with anarchy in industry! Down with capitalists who engage in lockouts!

Long live workers' supervision and organization of industry!

It's time to end the war! Let the Soviet of deputies announce just conditions of peace!

Neither a separate peace with Wilhelm, nor secret treaties with French and English capitalists!

Bread! Peace! Freedom!

LEAFLET 12

"The All-Russian Congress of Soviets Proclamation Opposing a Demonstration"

June 10, 1917

Soldier and worker comrades!

The Bolshevik Party is calling you out onto the street.

Their appeal was prepared without the knowledge of the Soviet of Workers' and Soldiers' Deputies, the All-Russian Congress, the Soviet of Peasants' Deputies, or any other socialist parties. It rang out right at the critical moment when the All-Russian Congress called upon worker comrades of Vyborg district to remember that any demonstrations during these days can harm the cause of the revolution. Comrades, on behalf of millions of workers, peasants, and soldiers in the rear and at the front we say to you:

Don't do what they are calling upon you to do.

At this critical moment, they are calling upon you to go onto the street to demand the overthrow of the Provisional Government, which the All-Russian [Soviet] Congress only just recognized as necessary to support.

Those who call you out cannot help but know that bloody riots may arise from your peaceful demonstration. Knowing your dedication to the revolutionary cause, we say to you:

They are calling upon you to demonstrate in favor of the revolution, but we know that hidden counterrevolutionaries want to make use of your demonstration.

We know that counterrevolutionaries eagerly await the moment when internecine war in the ranks of revolutionary democratic forces will make it possible for them to crush the revolution.

Comrades!

In the name of all Soviets of Workers' and Soldiers' Deputies, the Soviet of Peasants' Deputies, armies in action, and socialist parties, we say to you:

Not one company, regiment, or group of workers should be on the street.

There should not be even one demonstration today.

A great struggle still confronts us.

When counterrevolutionary danger actually threatens Russian freedom, we will call upon you.

Disorderly demonstrations are the downfall of the revolution.

Conserve your forces.

Act in concert with all revolutionary Russia.

All-Russian Congress of Soviets of Workers' and Soldiers' Deputies
Executive Committee of the Petrograd Soviet
of Workers' and Soldiers' Deputies
Executive Committee of the All-Russian Soviet of Peasant Deputies
Organizational Committee of the RSDRP [Menshevik]
Central Committee of the Party of Socialist Revolutionaries
Central Committee of the Bund
Central Committee of the Laborite Group [Trudoviks]
Ukrainian fraction of the All-Russian Congress
Fraction of United Internationalists of SD Bolsheviks
and Mensheviks of the All-Russian Congress
Military Section under the Organizational Committee and
Committee of the Petrograd Organization of the RSDRP[77]

LEAFLETS 13 AND 14
Responses to the July Days Uprising

In the days of July 3–7, 1917, a protest movement of workers and soldiers in Petrograd was repelled by military and police attacks, with hundreds of casualties. The July Uprising or July Days came about due to the failure of the Russian military offensive in June, a worsening of the crisis in Petrograd's food and fuel supply, and a crisis of confidence in the government after two Liberal (Kadet) ministers resigned over their opposition to Ukrainian autonomy.

In the wake of the offensive's collapse, mass unrest arose in the Russian army, which could no longer fight effectively. The uprising began among soldiers in the Petrograd garrison who feared transfer to the front, but also involved workers already on strike over low wages. Workers and soldiers demanded "all power to the soviets" and raised other radical slogans.

Members of the Bolshevik Military Organization, anarchists, and Left Social Revolutionaries encouraged the soldiers' revolt. The Central Committee of the Bolsheviks originally opposed the uprising, but quickly changed its position to one of support after tens of thousands of demonstrators surrounded the Tauride Palace, where the Soviet met.

The defeat of the July movement temporarily checked the revolution's impetus, as the Provisional Government drove the Bolshevik movement semi-underground and arrested Leon Trotsky and many other revolutionary leaders.[78]

The first document below represents the position toward the uprising of the moderate socialists, who then held a majority in the soviets. The second document provides the Bolshevik point of view.

LEAFLET 13

"Protests Strike Blows against Our Brothers at the Front"

July 3–4, 1917

To all workers and soldiers of the city of Petrograd.

Soldier and worker comrades!

Despite the clearly expressed will of all socialist parties without exception, unknown people are calling upon you to go out armed onto the street. This is how they propose that you should protest against the disbanding of regiments which dishonored themselves at the front by criminally abandoning their duty to the revolution.

As the authorized representatives of all Russia's revolutionary democratic forces, we declare to you: army and front organizations demanded the disbandment of regiments at the front, which was carried out by the order of War Minister Comrade A. F. Kerensky, whom we chose. The protests in defense of the disbanded regiments strike blows against our brothers who are spilling their blood at the front.

We remind the soldier comrades that not one military unit has the right to go out armed without the permission of the commander-in-chief, who is acting in full agreement with us.

We declare that all those who violate this decision during this so critical time for Russia are traitors and enemies of the revolution.

We will implement this decision by all the means at our disposal.

Bureau of the All-Russian Central Executive Committee
of the Soviet of Workers' and Soldiers' Deputies
Bureau of the All-Russian Executive Committee
of Soviets of Peasants' Deputies
July 3–4, 1917

LEAFLET 14
"Let the All-Russian Soviet Take All Power"
July 3–4, 1917

Worker and soldier comrades of Petrograd! Given that the counter-revolutionary bourgeoisie has obviously come out against the revolution, let the All-Russian Soviet of Workers', Soldiers' and Peasants' Deputies take all power into its hands.

This is the will of the revolutionary population of Petrograd, which has the right to bring its will, by means of peaceful and organized demonstration, to the attention of the Executive Committees of the All-Russian Soviet of Workers', Soldiers', and Peasants' Deputies, which is now in session.

Long live the will of the revolutionary workers and soldiers!

Long live the power of the soviets!

The coalition government suffered failure. Unable to carry out the tasks for which it was created, it collapsed. The revolution faces enormous and extremely difficult tasks. A new authority is needed that would, in unity with the revolutionary proletariat, the revolutionary army, and the revolutionary peasantry, resolutely fortify the people's conquests. Only the soviets of workers', soldiers', and peasants' deputies can be such an authority.

Yesterday, the revolutionary garrison of Petrograd and workers came out to advance the slogan "All power to the Soviet!" We call for the transformation of this movement, which flared up in the regiments and in the factories, into the peaceful, organized expression of the will of all of worker, soldier, and peasant Petrograd.

Central Committee of the Russian
Social Democratic Workers' Party (RSDRP)
Petersburg Committee of the RSDRP
Interdistrict Committee of the RSDRP
Military Organization of the CC RSDRP
Commission of the Workers' Section of the
Soviet of Workers' and Soldiers' Deputies
July 3–4, 1917[79]

LEAFLETS 15 AND 16
The Bolsheviks Retreat in Order to Advance

The Bolsheviks responded to the July Days repression by calling on working people to ignore provocations and expose rightist slanders.

After Provisional Government propaganda convinced sufficient numbers of soldiers and other citizens that the Germans had paid the Bolsheviks to undermine the Russian war effort, support for the July demonstrations began to falter and fade. Violent outbursts during the demonstrations also helped to discredit them. Having summoned loyal troops to Petrograd, the government cracked down on the Bolshevik Party by closing their newspaper Pravda, *arresting many leading Bolsheviks, and sending troops to occupy their party headquarters. Lenin fled Petrograd in disguise and went underground in Finland.*[80]

The two appeals below—both dated July 5, 1917—represent the Bolsheviks' responses to the developing situation.

LEAFLET 15

"Don't Yield to Provocation"

July 5, 1917

Calm and restraint!

Workers, soldiers!

The demonstration of July 3–4 has ended. You told the ruling classes what your goals are. Dark and criminal forces are casting a shadow over your demonstration by calling for blood to be shed. Together with you and all revolutionary Russia, we mourn for the recently fallen sons of the people. Responsibility for the victims falls upon the underground enemies of the revolution. But they did not and will not succeed in distorting the meaning of our demonstration.

Now it remains to wait and see what response your appeal, "All Power to the Soviets," will meet across the entire country. The demonstration has ended. Days of persistent agitation to enlighten the backward masses and to enlist the provinces to join our side are beginning anew.

Worker and soldier comrades! We call upon you to be calm and practice restraint. Don't give the malicious forces of reaction any reason to accuse you of violent acts. Don't yield to provocation. Don't come out onto the streets or engage in any clashes.

Worker comrades! Return peacefully to your workbenches.

Soldier comrades! Remain peacefully in your units.

Everything that exists is working in our favor. Victory will be ours. There is no need for rash acts.

Steadfastness, restraint, and calm are our watchword.

Central Committee of the Russian Social
Democratic Workers' Party (RSDRP)
Petersburg Committee of the RSDRP
Military Organization of the RSDRP
Interdistrict Committee of the United
Social Democratic Internationalists
July 5, 1917

LEAFLET 16
"Slander Should Be Exposed"
July 5, 1917

To the people of Petrograd! To workers! To soldiers! To all honest citizens! Slander should be exposed! Take the slanderers to court!

An unprecedented accusation has been lodged against Comrade Lenin—the charge that he received and still receives money from German sources for his agitation. Newspapers have already aired this monstrous slander. Already we see underground leaflets referring to the former deputy [Grigory] Alexinsky. They already print calls to murder Bolsheviks. Deceived soldiers are already circulating, from hand to hand, lists of people who may be exterminated.

The goal is clear. The counterrevolutionary forces want to use the simplest means to deprive the revolution of a leader, to sow discord among the masses and to stir them up against the most popular leaders—the meritorious worthy fighters for revolution.

We declare: All information about Comrade Lenin's financial ties or other ties to the ruling classes of Germany is a lie and slander.

Alexinsky, who initiated the case, is a notorious slanderer, who has accused many people of having been bribed by the Germans. In France, a union of journalists from Russia, Britain, Italy, and neutral countries has already condemned him for dishonesty and malicious slander and excluded him from all the democratic organizations of Paris. He was not admitted to the Petrograd Soviet of Workers' and Soldiers' Deputies.

We demand from the Provisional Government and from the Central Executive Committee of Soviets of Workers' and Soldiers' Deputies an immediate, public investigation of all the circumstances surrounding the mean conspiracy by pogromists and hired slanderers against the honor and lives of the leaders of the working class.

This entire affair needs to be cleared up. This investigation will convince all the people that there is not even one stain on Comrade Lenin's revolutionary honor.

Take the slanderers and distributors of slander to court! Subject pogromists and liars to public ridicule!

Central Committee of the RSDRP
July 5, 1917[81]

The leaflets translated above were taken from Alexander Shlyapnikov's published memoirs about the 1917 Revolution, which break off in the month of July. Subsequently, Shlyapnikov led the Petrograd Metalworkers' Union to successfully negotiate a wage rates agreement with factory owners. Part IV of this book provides translations of selected documents about the wage rates negotiations. Shlyapnikov also participated in organizing worker militias, which are discussed in the next section, part III.

PART III
Arming Militants: Worker Militias and the Red Guard

Created by the Petrograd Soviet of Workers' and Soldiers' Deputies on February 28, 1917, the worker militias of Petrograd replaced disintegrating tsarist police forces. They were meant to safeguard property and maintain order, but Bolsheviks wanted to broaden their agenda. Moderate and radical socialists differed over whether the worker militias should advance revolutionary goals. The Soviet attempted to exert more restraint over worker militias in March and April 1917. It ordered the worker militias to unite with the civil militia of Petrograd, but many units did not do so. Meanwhile, Bolsheviks and other radicals decided to create a worker "guard," which would be more revolutionary than the worker "militias." They preferred to call it a "red guard." By August 1917, the Red Guard had superseded the worker militias.[82]

1.

Project for Party Militias Drawn Up by the Petersburg Committee of the RSDRP(b) in Mid-April 1917

Shlyapnikov states in his memoirs that the following was the basis for the subsequent decree of the Vyborg Soviet, with important exceptions. Shlyapnikov objected to the militias being party-based, for he thought that organizing them through soviets would allow the inclusion of workers sympathetic to the Bolsheviks but not yet members of the party. He favored launching worker militias in those Petrograd district soviets in which Bolsheviks prevailed.[83]

* * *

1. To guarantee that the party can work openly against counterrevolutionary encroachments from the direction of both the Provisional Government and counterrevolutionary bourgeois parties, the Petersburg Committee creates its own social democratic worker Red Guard (militia), which is composed of district detachments.

The Red Guard comprises conscious, armed, strictly disciplined riflemen detachments and engineering-technical detachments for special assignments.

In peacetime, the Red Guard's sphere of activity is to protect assemblies, meetings, and demonstrations. In wartime, the Red Guard should carry out partisan struggle against the opponent.

2. District militias are organized in each district toward the same goal (division into districts is essential):

    a) district militias are divided into subdistrict detachments;

    b) there are no fewer than three detachments in each militia, but beyond that the number of detachments depends on the geographic and organizational size of the district;

c) detachments are divided into hundreds;

d) there are three hundreds in a detachment; and

e) hundreds are divided into tens.

3. The ten, the hundred, the detachment, the militia, and the guard have their own elected directors. The choice of directors occurs in the following way:

The ten elects the director of the ten. The directors of the tens elect the hundredth from among them. The hundredths elect the director of the detachment. The directors of the detachments elect the commander of the militia. The commanders of the militia elect the commander of the Red Guard.

Directors are replaced in sequence.

4. Councils (soviets) with a deciding vote are elected to serve under the commanders of the Red Guard, militias, and detachments.

5. When military action begins, all power transfers to the chief and orders proceed exclusively from him.

2.

Alexander Shlyapnikov, "Worker Guard"

Based on the February 28, 1917, resolution of the Petrograd Soviet of Workers' and Soldiers' Deputies about organizing a "district militia," the Vyborg District Soviet of Workers' and Soldiers' Deputies decided to transform the militia into a "Worker Guard."

* * *

Draft Statute of the "Worker Guard"

Goals:

The Worker Guard sets as its tasks:

1. [*Point #1 is absent in the draft Shlyapnikov quoted in full in his memoirs,* Semnadtsatyi god—Ed.]

2. Struggle against the ruling classes' counterrevolutionary schemes that hurt the people's interests.

3. Armed defense of all gains by the working class.

4. Protect the life, safety, and property of all citizens, without distinctions as to sex, age, and nationality.[84]

Composition:

Any working man or woman can be a member of the Worker Guard, if he or she is a member of a socialist party or a member of a trade union, on the recommendation or election of a general meeting of the factory or craft shop.

Plan of Organization:

1. All members of the Worker Guard are united into Tens and have at their head an elected Tenth.

2. Tens compose Hundreds, at the head of which are Hundredths.

3. Ten Hundreds compose a Battalion of the Worker Guard, with an elected chief and two assistants at its head.

4. Hundredths of each battalion, together with assistants of the battalion chief, and under the chief's chairmanship, form a Battalion Soviet.

5. The Battalion Soviet receives all instructions and orders from the five-member Soviet of the Worker Guard, which is elected by the District Soviet of Workers' and Soldiers' Deputies. The five members include a chair, two assistants for the chair, and two members.

6. While serving, members of the Worker Guard observe strict, ideologically conscious, comradely discipline.

Armaments:

The War Ministry is obligated to pay for the Worker Guard's armaments, which consist of rifles, revolvers, and similar equipment.

Resources:

The resources of the "Worker Guard" consist of:

1. special collections and donations, including from enterprises;

2. revenue from the city government's resources, which will be designated for the city's policing needs.

A general assembly of the Vyborg District Soviet of Workers' and Soldiers' Deputies has accepted this draft. The Soviet charged its compilers to develop a detailed "Instructions to the Worker Guard" in the spirit of the principles laid out in the "Draft Statute."[85]

3.

Anonymous, "About the Red Guard"

A statement about the Red Guard published in Rabochaia gazeta, *a Menshevik newspaper.*

* * *

We already pointed out in one of the first issues of our newspaper that the arming of a people's militia is not now on the revolutionary agenda, because the army has come over to the people's side and stands guard over the revolution's achievements.

As one might have expected, the Leninists took exactly the opposite position. They stubbornly repeat that workers need to be armed and they create the impression that danger threatens the revolution if the entire people are not armed. They talk very much about the unity of soldiers and workers and even propose to transfer all government power to soviets of workers' and soldiers' deputies. At the same time, they insistently summon workers now to universal arms, as if they are instilling in them distrust toward the revolutionary army.

Here, as in all their demagogic activity, they require only the transitory success of a revolutionary phrase. They know perfectly well that a worker militia or "red guard" could not resist the army, if there would be conflict between workers and the army. On the contrary, as long as there will be unity between workers and the army, such a militia is unnecessary and even dangerous.

But as always in such cases, workers who possess a revolutionary mood but insufficient political education follow the revolutionary phrase rather than the voice of reason.

In Petrograd, as the result of Leninist agitation, "red guards" numbering in the thousands have already formed. They train, they hold meetings, and they organize armed demonstrations. A special psychology is created of the sad memory of "armed detachments," the need for something to display their "fighting spirit" and bravery. The revolutionary atmosphere now is one of unprecedented political freedom. Currently there is no serious danger for the revolution, yet a fighting organization is being created with all the peculiar characteristics of such an organization.

The Leninists know perfectly well that the people have never achieved victory over the army in any revolution. Never before in any revolution has there been such a formidable fighting force as the army of millions, which is on the side of the people. They also know many other things. They know that the general call to arms is now an empty phrase, because there are no weapons, if they are not taken from the barracks.

But what is all this to them? Let all the petty bourgeoisie become embittered against these bellicose, warlike preparations by separate groups of workers, whom no one is preparing to attack. Let distrust be implanted among some of the troops—distrust which actual enemies of the revolution then can easily use.

For now, it's "Let's make some noise, guys," but later on it will be "After us the deluge."[86]

4.

A. Belenin (Alexander Shlyapnikov), "About the 'Red Guard'"

Writing under his pseudonym, Shlyapnikov here asserts the Bolshevik defense of the Red Guard.

★ ★ ★

The city's worker districts have placed on the agenda the creation of an organized "worker militia" and "red or worker guard." This business has elicited a whole stream of newspaper articles and notices. The yellow bourgeois press had yet another opportunity to raise a wail about anarchy.

There is nothing surprising in this. During the great days of revolution, the tasks of the bourgeois press are to sow panic, spread discord, and breed strife among revolutionary soldier and worker ranks. Everyone knows this. But the matter takes another turn when voices from the circles of democratic forces join the chorus about "anarchy." I mean the article "About the Red Guard," which appeared in *Rabochaia gazeta*, no. 43. This venerable newspaper declares that presently the revolutionary agenda does not include "arming the people." Therefore, it states, efforts of workers to organize a militia are only "Leninist" intrigues. The Kadet *Sovremennik* supports the same position.

The bourgeois press tries to counterpoise the "red guard" to the revolutionary army. But not one worker would set his rifles and pistols against the powerful equipment of the army. Workers are not attempting to organize their army for this. Soldiers have understood this better than have politicians sitting in their offices. Anyone who was in the ranks of the revolutionary people on February 27 remembers how joyfully soldiers helped their brothers the workers arm themselves.

At that time the Soviet approved a project for arming ten workers out of every hundred and thus creating a "worker militia."

The natural desire to give all their strength to the cause of revolution shows in the efforts of a broad range of workers to organize their own armed forces. Workers have still not forgotten the days of February 23–26 and they know how bad it is to be armed only with enthusiasm.

Besides this, other considerations force workers to organize a "red guard." Everyone can clearly grasp the consideration that upon the end of war, the entire Petrograd garrison or a significant part of it will abandon the capital.

The second and most important is dissatisfaction with the existing militia organization. All workers are speaking out against the creation of professional "policemen" who are cut off from the life of laborers. Workers see a dangerous abnormality in the existence of militia institutions detached from their professional interests. They propose creating a broader organization of armed forces, which, alongside their work, would take turns at guard duty and other services.

Izvestia in no. 52 justly points out the harm of independent "fighting units," and in this case, it agrees with the general opinion of workers. The Red Guard organizers really did err when they created this important organization without liaising with [Petrograd city] district soviets of workers' and soldiers' deputies, which are charged with the task of organizing a "people's militia."

Izvestia should recommend to them the path taken by the Vyborg District Soviet of Workers' and Soldiers' Deputies, in which Bolsheviks, Mensheviks, and SRs unanimously confirmed the statutes given to the editors of *Izvestia*.

Revolutionary working people cannot be forced by any article or resolution to give up arms. It's possible to usher in disorder and enable the existence of uncontrolled, irresponsible armed bands. Soviets and parties should and can struggle against this by assuming the initiative in this serious business.[87]

PART IV

The Economic Struggle: Documents of the Petrograd Metalworkers' Union

Although renowned as among the most activist of Russia's workers, Petrograd metalworkers lagged in forming a citywide union in 1917. This was due to their early preoccupation with political activism that year, the preference of many metalworkers for the factory committee form of organization, and craft union loyalties. The Petrograd Metalworkers' Union was finally formed on April 23, 1917, and its central board comprised Alexander Shlyapnikov (a Bolshevik), Alexei Gastev (an unaffiliated socialist who would join the Bolsheviks), and I. G. Volkov (a Menshevik).

The union's early activity included mediation between workers and owners and assisting the unemployed in finding work through labor exchanges. Its leadership settled upon a uniform wage rates system as a goal that could attract workers into the union and unify them. Workers were dissatisfied with their wages, which were not keeping up with rising food and fuel prices. This tactic proved successful in strengthening unions, although it nearly foundered in the wake of the failed July Days uprising.

The All-Russian Metalworkers' Union was formed in late June 1917, but before it could fully function, unions had to be built up in Russia's provinces. In October 1917, major conferences of metalworkers' union organizations were held in Moscow and Kharkov. The Moscow conference, held on October 6, 1917, revealed the readiness of unionized metalworkers for soviet power, nationalization of large industry and transport, and implementation of workers' supervision over production.

1.

Resolutions of Petrograd Metalworkers' Representatives about the Political and Economic Situation in Russia

Summer 1917

1a. The following resolution was adopted after detailed discussion by a meeting of representatives from seventy-three metalworking factories with leaders of the Petrograd Metalworkers' Union, held at the Putilov factory in late June 1917.

* * *

The meeting of factory committees with the participation of: 1) representatives of the Central Council of Factory Committees, 2) the Central Bureau of Trade Unions, 3) the Board of the Union of Metalworkers, 4) socialist parties, and likewise with the participation of factory and shop committees of Putilov factory, having discussed the coming out of Putilov factory workers in defense of the demands they have presented, declares: 1) that the cause of the Putilov workers is the cause of the entire Petrograd proletariat; 2) that all metalworkers present similar demands through their trade union to the Society of Factory Owners, and likewise to the government departments; 3) and that a partial economic demonstration under present conditions can entail unorganized political struggle by Petrograd workers. For these reasons, Putilov workers are advised to restrain their legitimate indignation against the behavior of the ministers, who are dragging out the resolution of conflict by all the means at their disposal. The meeting's participants consider it necessary to prepare forces for joint demonstrations very soon.

Together with that, the Putilovtsy [Putilov workers] are asked to transfer their demands to the Union of Metalworkers, so that it may negotiate them with employers and government departments as part of a common wage rates system, and in the future to make their steps on this matter agree with the decision of the all-city delegates' assembly of the Union of Metalworkers.

Moreover, the meeting of factory committees of Petrograd and of shop committees of the Putilov factory supposes that even if wage increases are achieved, then the currently uninterrupted growth of prices for food and rent would reduce this gain to nothing. Therefore, resolute struggle is needed to establish worker supervision (control) over production and distribution. This in its turn demands passage of power into the hands of soviets of workers, soldiers, and peasant deputies.[88]

1b. The following resolution is from a later meeting, when metalworkers' delegates objected to factory owners' insistence that they guarantee productivity.

* * *

1. Professional worker organizations [trade unions] cannot undertake to guarantee for capitalists a certain amount of profit, which depends not only on labor productivity in each enterprise but also on the general industrial conjuncture.

2. Employers, toward obviously counterrevolutionary ends, directly sabotage production by taking measures which reduce the productivity of labor and the productivity of enterprises.

3. By opposing point 4 to all the remaining demands of the wage rates agreement, the Society of Factory Owners obviously tries to make the working class shoulder responsibility for the disorganization of production, which employers intentionally provoke and carry out themselves. Thus, the delegates' assembly of the Union of Metalworkers protests against these actions by the capitalists and exposes them to broad masses of the population.

Along with that, keeping in mind:

1. that the imperialist war has created such a situation for the country now that the working class and the trade unions, as its militant organizers, are confronted with new tasks of directly supervising and organizing production;

2. that the working class has a direct interest in preserving and developing the country's productive forces and in expanding production;

3. that the labor productivity of each worker in each enterprise depends both on his level of training and how much effort he exerts in his labor, and on the technical, administrative, and similar conditions in each enterprise.

Taking all this into account, we also suppose that in order for workers' labor and enterprises' productivity to be correctly regulated in the interests of the working class and of the entire country, power in the country needs to pass into the hands of soviets of workers', soldiers', and peasants' deputies, which will permit victory over the capitalist bourgeoisie's disorganization and sabotage of production. Therefore, the delegates' assembly of the Metalworkers' Union resolves to propose our own point 4 of the wage rates agreement to that point proposed by the Society of Factory Owners. Our point 4 is the workers' demand that wage rates valuation commissions would establish norms for the productivity of workers' labor and that they would guarantee such working conditions, technology, and other conditions in the enterprise which determine the productivity of both labor and the enterprise.

The delegates' assembly appoints the Board to negotiate point 4 with the Society of Factory Owners and it declares that the Union of Metalworkers is ready to support its demands with all its strength, when this will be politically necessary and convenient. At the same time, it emphasizes that at the current time no enterprises may be permitted to carry out individual demonstrations without the Board having discussed this in advance, for such can only disorganize and weaken the forces of the working class.[89]

2.

Alexander Shlyapnikov, "Our Wage Rates Agreement"

Petrograd Metalworkers' Union leaders and factory owners signed a wage rates agreement on August 7, 1917, and it was implemented in factories in spite of the economic crisis. Although inflation quickly outpaced its rates, the agreement became a model for other industrial unions to follow. The failure of the wage rates agreement, however, to address fundamental inequities encouraged some trade union leaders and members to see a solution to their problems in a revolution that would transfer power to the soviets.[90]

The following article by Petrograd and All-Russian Metalworkers' Union Chair Alexander Shlyapnikov begins by surveying wage rates work in Petrograd in 1917 before the Union of Metalworkers assumed responsibility for it. Shlyapnikov's essay sets the negotiations in the context of a worsening economic crisis and explains the union's methods of preparing for negotiations. He analyzes the relationship between the roles of unions, capitalists, and government in the negotiations and the impact of the failed July Days uprising upon the negotiations. He also addresses the key points of disagreement between unions and capitalists in relation to the wage rates agreement and the pressure brought upon negotiations by worker delegates and workers on the shop floor. Finally, the essay projects how the wage rates commissions would operate in practice in the factories. The article was published in the first issue of the Metalworkers' Union journal Metallist. *Although dated August 17, 1917, the journal was published with a delay and may have appeared only on the eve of the October Revolution. The dates in the article are based on the old Julian calendar, which lagged thirteen days behind the Gregorian calendar used in the West.*

* * *

Trade unions were born in the throes of revolution. Although strong in spirit, they were still organizationally weak. To their lot fell the difficult and crucial task for the time of directing proletarian spontaneity by means of economic struggle.

When the Union of Metalworkers first officially opened, it had to contend with a large, already existing movement to raise wages. This movement was extremely disorganized. Workers ran from one factory to another and from one district to another. Independently of each other, factory committees collected information about the size of wages.

Conflicts grew daily. When one factory was won over, then consequently a neighboring one would resolve to come out. Very successful gains would give rise to new conflict and new demands upon the first factory.

Everyone recognized how abnormal the situation was. Those who sensed it first were the ones who had to introduce some regularity or systematic planning into this struggle. A massive flood of similar demands spoke of the need for a common means of struggle. This was found.

The Board of the Metalworkers' Union decided to work out a common wage rates agreement for the metals industry of the Petrogradsky district. This made it possible at one go to suspend all individual protests demanding wage increases, and to channel this movement in an organized way. The entire "metals family" of Petrograd responded keenly to the idea of a uniform wage rates agreement, which was very significant in an organizational sense, because it created discipline among the entire proletariat of the metals factories and united it around the union.

For more than two months, the union successfully restrained around 180 factories, mills, and workshops, including the giant Putilov factory, from going on strike.

The present time appears to be very unfavorable for wage rates norms. The fluctuating rate of the ruble and rising food prices are complicating factors, for they make the value of a wage rates agreement rather relative. But its implementation even in such abnormal conditions is an enormous advantage for the proletarians of the steel industry, for at one go it puts an end to the endless division and subdivision of workers according to their wages. The wage rates agreement will bring all professions and specialties into a structured framework and will remove from employers the power to arbitrarily evaluate labor according to order of precedence or parochialism.[91]

Usually a wage rates agreement can prevent wage decreases in times of economic depression and crisis, but that is when there are no complications from war and its attendant ruin. You can't say this is true in our time, because the uninterrupted growth of the cost of living radically undermines any guarantees. However, a systematically implemented wage rates agreement makes it possible to painlessly resolve all the inauspicious aspects. When the norms of an agreement fall too far behind reality, it undergoes review, with employers' consent, of course.

To work out the wage rates agreement, the Union of Metalworkers created a special rates valuation commission, which included representatives from all districts of the city. The rates commission, which was composed exclusively of workers, faced the rather complicated and critical work of defining the norms of the agreement, which depended on placing numerous professions and specialties into groups and categories. The task was difficult, for there was neither any experience in this area nor any statistics to serve as resources.

Members of the rates commission had to do the work themselves to collect prices of consumer goods and compose lists of wages from the city districts. The union had to solve in a matter of days all problems connected to wage rates. In Western Europe, they worked out solutions to these problems over many years. Despite unfavorable conditions, Petrograd metalworkers emerged honorably from this work. Prominent leaders of Petrograd's industry joined the Wage Rates Commission of the Mechanical Department of the Society of Factory Owners. They accepted all basic principles for constructing a wage rates agreement and the division of metals industry workers into four production groups. Any divergence of opinion with the Society of Factory Owners was on individual points, which were unconnected with the general plan.

The rates commission's work ended as the second half of June began. Right away the Board [of the Union of Metalworkers] instructed the author of this article, as chair of the Board and as a member of the rates commission, to enter negotiations with the Society of Factory Owners.

The Mechanical Department of the Society of Factory Owners very quickly agreed to our proposal. The situation in the factories greatly worried metals industry leaders, so their organization, despite being of the Old Regime and militantly anti-worker, entered negotiations with us. The first session was held on June 22. We will publish all the materials we have about it.

The negotiations proceeded rather quickly. Full agreement was achieved on the last points of the agreement, although not without frictions. A rather large "hitch" in the negotiations occurred when our Delegates' Council indiscriminately rejected all proposals from the Mechanical Department of the Society of Factory Owners, especially the point about a certain guarantee of productivity. Soon we corrected this mistake. The All-City Delegates' Council passed a resolution about output norms.

This resolution knocked the ground out from under the feet of the enemies of the working class, who had accused us of desiring only minimum wages, without giving in return a minimum of labor. The union loudly declared that by struggling for raising wages and for the best labor conditions and against the ruling classes' predatory misappropriation of the work force and of labor, it supports developing labor productivity.

Judging from the pace of negotiations, we thought that we would end all our work and conclude an agreement in early July. On the evening of July 3, however, armed demonstrations in the city interrupted our meeting. We could reassemble only on July 12, when we received news that the General Assembly of Factory Owners decided not to make concessions. It was clear that that the policy "of strong authority" and struggle with "anarchy" encouraged the ringleaders of the metals industry.

To the meeting on July 12, the industrialists sent many new people, having removed some of the "liberals." Everything pointed to their desire to give "resolute rebuff." Toward this decisive step, they zigzagged and caviled over various individual points of our agreement. However, they failed to create delays this time. Having answered all quibbles in the same way, which was that the union would come to an understanding, we approached the main thing, which was the matter of rates.

We disagreed with the industrialists greatly over wage norms by groups and categories. Based on the variety in our metals industry, we proposed to accept in the agreement only one minimum wage, which was in the third category of each group, while allowing local conditions to determine the high mark for the first and second categories. The industrialists greatly opposed this view. They declared the need for definitions in all three categories. Their point of view was accepted by the interdepartmental conference and by the Ministry of Labor.

There was much dispute over high marks of rates. The industrialists relatively easily accepted rates for highly skilled workers, but the lower the degree of training, the stricter and stingier they became. This is understandable. Indeed, highly skilled workers in the metals industry compose a relatively small group of people. *Machinisme* and automatism,[92] together with a wide division of labor, make it possible to break up the most precise and complicated work into the simplest operations, which unskilled men and women workers can fulfill. The further you go, the greater and more numerous become this group of semiskilled semi-specialists, and the more stubbornly the capitalists refuse to satisfy their demands.

Our rates for the unskilled elicited a roar of exclamations and protests. The capitalists saw a danger to industry in paying for the labor of unskilled workers and women. Even up to now our capitalists have remained true to this old worn-out method—to declare the working class's most fair and equitable demands to be fatal for industry.

At a time when the cost of living is unusually high, they considered it too much to pay eight rubles to an unskilled male worker and six rubles, eighty kopecks to a woman worker for eight hours of work. They allotted seventy-five to eighty kopecks per hour to each man and only sixty-five kopecks to women. This was at a time when the market "price," that is the wage for unskilled workers, was higher than that set by our wage rates system, because there was a great demand for working hands for [military] field work. At the same time, individual factory owners demanded laborers through our Unemployment Bureau at wages of eight to ten rubles for an eight-hour working day.

The metals industrialists' stubbornness about this matter resulted from the pressure which the entire Society of Factory Owners placed on the Mechanical Department. The capitalists understood very well that if the demands of the unskilled workers of the metals industry were satisfied, then on the next day the textile workers, leather workers, and workers in other branches of production would demand the very same thing.

Thus, the wage rates agreement of the metalworkers became all-proletarian. The unskilled metalworkers' demand became the demand of all low-paid workers in all of Petrograd industry.

When the Society of Factory Owners refused to accept the proposed norms of payment for unskilled labor, this put a general strike of metalworkers on the agenda. The conditions of the time made it unnecessary to resort to this. The suggestion of the Ministry of Labor made temporary satisfaction possible, although it was a compromise and so forth.

The Departmental Conference's halfhearted compromise settlement, which the Ministry of Labor supports, does not satisfy us. We based our demand for payment of unskilled labor on a precise determination of the rising cost of living. Thus, the earnings of the unskilled were the subsistence minimum, below which one would starve. The Ministry of Labor, therefore, takes great responsibility upon itself when it lowers our rates. We expected from it the quickest resolution of the problem about a living wage for unskilled workers of our district.

Finally, negotiations have ended. In just a few days, we and the Society of Factory Owners will sign the agreement. When our agreement enters force, the most important part of our wage rates activity will be transferred to the worksites. Serious work to implement the agreement should begin in the sites of the workshops and the factories. In carrying out this work, our comrades should display all their energy, farsightedness, and ingenuity.

First, the most serious attention should be turned to the institution of local factory or mill "rates commissions." Our union delegates, together with factory committees, should determine the composition of the factory rates commission, proceeding from the interests of the entire workforce of the given factory. The rates commissions should not be too cumbersome. They should consist of representatives of the largest professions, by which should not be understood the narrow specializations of various workshops, because such an interpretation would lead to a very big, unwieldy organization.

For example, let's take a midsized Petrograd factory with the following workshops: 1) mechanical, 2) bellows or rolling, 3) casting, and 4) pattern making and joinery. The rates commission will be composed of [about six people]. Two should be from the mechanical shop. One of these should be an experienced lathe operator who can work at all work benches, including planing, milling, and rolling, and the other should be a good fitter, who understands all the given factory's work. From the bellows, there should be one experienced blacksmith. From steel rolling, one experienced rolling mill operator is sufficient. An experienced molder from casting who knows the entire foundry business is needed. One senior joiner-carpenter–pattern maker, who can perform all woodworking operations, is called for.

Such a rates commission, which the entire factory selects, can work, and can unify all shops. It will consider the interests of all workers of a given enterprise, not just those of individual specialties.

Comrades who are members of our union need to be elected to the rates commission. Their work to implement our agreement is very crucial. Therefore, they should be responsible not only to those who elected them, but also to the entire union. It follows that the rates commissions in enterprises need to compose a protocol for each election and to designate a deputy for each candidate. Case files about elections would be delivered to the union.

The term of office for the rates commission needs to be determined, so that there will not be reelections over trifles. Therefore, we propose to implement a half-year term of office. Besides that, our rates commissions need to be protected from unfair attacks at the worksites. It is very difficult to listen when workers curse those whom they've elected, for example members of "factory committees" and so forth, and often just over trifles. Comrades who will be dissatisfied with the rates commission should be advised to appeal directly to the union and not to pronounce judgment upon them without a court, in order not to introduce disorganization into our ranks.

The work of rates commissions at worksites will be complex and difficult. The employers will in many ways restrict the significance and meaning of individual points of the agreement. Workers should be ready to extract from the agreement the maximum use.

Likewise, it needs to be kept in mind that our wage rates agreement does not eliminate the basis of exploitation. It does not stall the growth of the cost of living, against which the entire struggle lies ahead of us. It does not open the doors into the kingdom of socialism. The wage rates agreement is an agreement between two parties who are in conflict. Therefore, it has force only inasmuch as the parties to the agreement are organized.

While implementing the wage rates agreement, we should not forget this. More than ever before, we should strengthen our union and summon everyone to come beneath its banner. The strength of our agreement lies only in the unity of all metalworkers. The guarantee for the success of the working class's struggle is only in unifying and organizing all its forces.[93]

3.

Alexander Shlyapnikov, "We Should Have Only One Union of Metalworkers"

August 17, 1917

Our union's organization is founded on [the principle of] the production association of all workers of the metals industry, without any distinction made among their professions, places of work, or conditions of work. The union strives to unite all exploited peoples of the world of metals, from apprentices to the most highly skilled workers. There should not be room in factories, among proletarians, for several organizations, since this threatens all workers with major complications and weakens their battle strength versus organized capital. Up to now, we have already had several attempts to divide our forces into small "unions." The "Union of Stokers and Assistants' appeared in the world. The "welders" organized into a special union. The "sorters," inspectors, pattern makers, and others are drawn into special associations. From a hundred specialties belonging to the metals industry, some have been found who did not consider it their duty to weld together their forces and their will with the entire metalworking family. Of course, in such a large family it's impossible to get by without some abnormality, but it needs to be eliminated as quickly as possible. The harm of separate organizations already begins to expose us. So, not long ago the "organized" welders of Gruntal workshop, numbering around eight people out of forty total workers at the enterprise, demanded wage increases. Having been denied, they declared a boycott on their jobs and went off to work at other factories. So, thirty other metalworker comrades, whose opinion the welders did not want to take into consideration, have been forced into unemployment. All organized, conscious members of our union should struggle against such isolated acts by individual professions which do not consider the interests of all workers of the enterprise or district.

Let all comrades keep this case in mind, when they will meet organizations parallel to our union in factories. Several unions cannot exist in one area of production without bringing harm to the common cause. Let's take the union of "stokers," which is now organizing. Can stokers independently, without joining together with other workers of those factories and mills where they work, improve their situation? No, a thousand times no! Stokers in our factories should go into one union with organized metalworkers. Let the stokers in textile factories merge with the textile unions, and so forth. Each profession should enter a common union for a given area of production. Electricians recognized this and join the Union of Metalworkers, while preserving in it a professional commission. All other small unions should follow this example. Metalworkers should have a single union, a single goal, and a single purpose.[94]

4.

Alexander Shlyapnikov, "Tasks of the Wage Rates Valuation Commissions"

October 1, 1917

According to point 23 in our wage rates agreement, rates valuation commissions are instituted in factories. Their main task is to implement the wage rates agreement. Their task is extraordinarily complex and crucial. First, they need to find the proper place for each diverse profession and specialty in each factory in the wage rates agreement and distribute them according to groups. This business is very difficult, because many specialties which exist under the currently reigning division of labor are not enumerated in the agreement. Further, the matter is complicated by a general aspiration toward belonging to a higher ranked group. However, with a serious attitude toward the work, it is possible to precisely determine the suitable place for any specialty. Points 1 and 2 of the "Guiding Principles" are the main thread for defining one or another profession. Besides that, the comparative method needs to be utilized. In those cases when some profession is difficult to define according to the first two points, the disputed specialty should be compared to another one which approximates it. A comparatively easier task is distribution by categories, since specialists relatively easily find a place for themselves. In questionable cases, especially in the first group, the question is easily decided through testing.

The valuation commissions likewise should intervene in choosing tests, so that tests would be normal, rather than excessively puzzling or cunning inventions of individual masters.

After distribution by groups and categories, the valuation commission should participate most actively in determining piece work rates. Piece work must be regarded with great attention. Output norms must be set not according to the worst worker's yield, but also not set according to the work of the best specialist. Experience in this matter is more valuable than any theoretical instructions and the valuation commissions on the sites will cope with this task. Given this, the valuation commissions should provide all sorts of incentives to workers' inventiveness, which will make work easier by application of various gadgets or devices.

When determining prices for piecework, one should proceed from the Wage Rates Norms. However, this does not mean that the worker's wage cannot be higher than the wage rate. Under piece rates, it would be completely normal if workers could develop productivity by percentages up to 25 percent higher than those set in the wage rates agreement. However, a maximum norm is needed, so that piece work should not turn into hard labor. There should be mutual agreement on this and supervision (control) by the workers themselves.

Besides those obligations enumerated, the worker part of the Factory Wage Rates Valuation Commission is responsible for maintaining the wage rates agreement and ensuring its observance in its entirety in all enterprises. The commission should make sure that not one worker is paid at a rate lower than that set by the agreement, wage rates are not lowered, workers work well, and so forth and the like.

All matters on which the worker part of the Rates Valuation Commission will not agree with the proprietors' side should be transferred to the Central Rates Valuation Commission, which, in accord with point 21, consists of representatives from both the Union of Metalworkers and the Society of Factory Owners. This Central Rates Valuation Commission will investigate all matters of dispute, both those based on interpreting the wage rates agreement and those arising during its practical application. The tasks of the worker part of the Central Rates Valuation Commission are great. The matter of wage rates on that scale on which we began it is something new not only in our country but also in Western Europe. Only through practical work can all its shortcomings be cleared up. This business now rests exclusively on the Central Rates Valuation Commission.[95]

5.

Alexander Shlyapnikov, "Once More about the Organization of Unions"

November 9, 1917

The trade union movement of Western Europe knows two main types of workers' organizations. One unites workers by profession or work specialties and the other brings them together according to the type of production in which they work. Between these two basic types are intermediate ones such as guilds, which unite several professions working in close contact. Examples are workers in foundries, in mechanical shops, in boiler houses, and so forth. Some organizations unite workers of a certain enterprise. The history of workers' organizational forms provides a complete, consummate picture of what is normal in developing proletarian organizations. Through many years of experience and cruel struggle, workers proceeded from small, specialized organizations all the way up to organizations representing areas of production, which are the last word in union technique. The old organizations subdivided the workforce into small, specialized groups. As a result, dozens of unions were represented at the same factory. The production manner of organization eliminates these shortcomings.

The plan for organizing according to type of production is built on uniting workers in the main branches of the economy. Instead of separate specialties or enterprises, the organization unites all the various specialties in all enterprises of a certain branch of production. This combines all proletarian forces, finishes off petty trade union dissension, and eliminates subdivision and organizational isolation. The old-fashioned type of organization and struggle are to the new technique and modern struggle as the blows of a blacksmith's hammer are to a mighty, hydraulic press, which squeezes in its stanchions the entire capitalist economic apparatus.

Everyone understands the advantage of large, production-type unions over handicrafts, guilds, and specialized professional organizations. Nevertheless, those of us in the Petrograd metalworking industry encounter narrow, specialized unions such as: stokers, welders, pattern makers, and woodworkers. In our time, all these specialties belong to various branches of production. As such, they are distributed in enterprises under the jurisdiction of metalworkers, leather workers, textile workers, and others. Isolated cells of the specialties indicated above are infected with guild prejudices. As the experience of the woodworkers' strike shows, they are not much inclined to consider the will and interests of most workers, even when a strike is announced. This presents a danger to all organizations, for it threatens to introduce disorganization and elements of discord into worker ranks.

The task of the Petrograd Council of Trade Unions is to curtail the guild and handicrafts unions. Its slogan should be one union for each branch of production. Workers of each mill and each factory should belong only to one union. There should not be several unions in the workplace. Workers can only improve their situation if all specialties are united. Separate professions cannot be permitted to use a "suitable moment" to present isolated, individual demands. Conscious circles of highly skilled metalworkers, such as fitters and turners, understand this wonderfully, so they renounce any separate demands. Most of the unskilled workers, who are most deprived and poorly paid, support this position. No matter how bad their situation, only in isolated cases do the unskilled present individual demands. It is chiefly small specialties like welders, of whom there are only about one thousand in Petrograd, which hold themselves aloof. Likewise, pattern makers, stokers, and draftsmen are few but are infected with the prejudice that their profession is qualitatively distinct from others. Therefore, they cannot combine to defend their interests by collaborating with other professions. This situation gives rise to the danger of disorganizing the entire struggle of the working class. Such a tendency can beget professional enmity in the worker milieu instead of the solidarity that is needed.

The lessons of the woodworkers' strike should not pass in vain. Individual professions cannot be permitted to work at cross-purposes to the general will of organized workers. Individual political intriguers, like those in the Stokers' Union, cannot be permitted to split the working class and poison one profession against another. Only through close collaboration, solidarity, and brotherhood can all professions defend their interests in a powerful union organized according to production area.[96]

6.

Alexander Shlyapnikov, "About the Conference of the Metalworkers' Union of Moscow Oblast"

November 9, 1917

The June [1917] meeting of Metalworkers' Union representatives at the All-Russian Conference of Trade Unions instructed the Temporary Committee of the All-Russian Metalworkers Union to devote a significant portion of its work to creating oblast-level unions, which it has done. In October, there were two conferences, one of which was in Kharkov and the other was in Moscow. Here, we only discuss the latter. . . .[97]

The conference accepted the following agenda:

1. Report by the Temporary Central Committee of the All-Russian Metalworkers' Union

2. Unions' economic policy and the current moment

3. Wage rates

4. Unemployment and measures to struggle against it

5. Organizational questions

The presenter on the first agenda item explained the grandiose task of unionizing almost a million metalworkers, which fell upon the Temporary Central Committee (CC) of the All-Russian Metalworkers' Union. In the provinces, the needs are enormous, and the leaders' forces are weak. Much is demanded of the center, but the CC does not have enough personnel to send for instructing those in the provinces. It mainly has shared the Petrograd Union's experience with remote provinces.

The conference's members expressed a common opinion of comradely gratitude toward their Temporary Center. The conference decided to support in any way it can the work to unite all metalworkers

of Russia and to strictly implement in the provinces the necessary
ten kopeck deduction [of dues].

The second point had two presenters, comrades Smidovich and
Kibrik.[98] Here like everywhere else, they offered two views on the
tasks of the working class and of the Russian Revolution. The question about power was the center of discussion. After prolonged and
very passionate debate, the conference accepted by 24 votes against
12 a resolution of the Moscow Soviet of Workers' and Soldiers' Deputies (the same which was accepted by the Petrograd Soviet), with
the following addenda:

> Subscribing to the resolution accepted by the Moscow Soviet of Workers'
> and Soldiers' Deputies on September 27, the oblast conference of metal-
> workers regards from its perspective that:
>
> 1. At a time of economic catastrophe, the Russian bourgeoisie
>   proved its completely reactionary nature as an economic force. It
>   proved not only its complete lack of interest in using the country's
>   production forces, but also its policy of economic sabotage, secret
>   lockouts, stoppages of production, and similar things, which
>   expose its disorganizing role. Obviously, it lacks the desire and
>   ability to extract the country from the economic collapse, into
>   which the world war led it.
>
> 2. In particular the metals industry of the Moscow region presently
>   is a cesspit through and through, in which joint-stock companies
>   speculate not to improve technology and production overall, but
>   to inflate stocks and pump out dividends. Under the regulation of
>   a stock exchange carrying out speculative adventures on military
>   and government orders, the Moscow metals industry fell into
>   an economic dead end, which was deepened by a collapse of all
>   economic life both artificially created and naturally developing.
>
> 3. Under such conditions, the heroic efforts of the working class are
>   needed to organize the country's entire economy. Trade unions
>   as workers' organizations should set their class politics, which
>   currently more than ever meets the demands of the overwhelming
>   majority of the population, in opposition to the bourgeoisie's
>   counterrevolutionary economic policy.

4. The working class should wage energetic struggle to radically change the government's principles for its economic policy. But the working class's current economic struggle more than any time before assumes the character of a political struggle for power. Only power built up by soviets of workers', soldiers', and peasant deputies, which as revolutionary democratic organizations represent those classes with an interest in developing and consolidating the gains of the Russian Revolution, can use production forces to the maximum extent possible in current conditions.

5. To avoid a complete economic crash, broad, centralized control (supervision) needs to be established immediately over the country's entire production, distribution, and banking. Supervisory bodies should have a majority of members comprising representatives from soviets of workers' deputies, trade unions, and factory committees.

6. In the conference's opinion, immediate nationalization of the largest syndicalized enterprises (for example: oil, coal, sugar, metals processing) and transport is a task of the government's economic policy that cannot be postponed. Likewise, financial policy should be changed radically in the direction of nationalizing banks.

7. The conference recommends that in the provinces, trade unions should implement workers' supervision (control) over production as soon as possible and should encourage initiative in doing so.

The author of this article presented about the wage rates agreement. I set forth the fundamentals of the Petrograd agreement. Likewise, I shared the Petrograd Union's experience of struggle for a wage rates agreement and for its implementation in the provinces afterwards. I pointed out that the stability of the wage rates agreement, especially of the wages secured by it, directly depends on general financial and economic policy. The Provisional Government's current policy undermines all of workers' wage gains. Therefore, one should not place any special hopes on collective agreement under existing conditions. All the imperfections of our time notwithstanding, wage rates agreements have enormous organizational significance. By campaigning for a wage rates agreement, the union touches upon the most painful places and the most backward strata of the working class and it chains to itself the interests of all professions. A vivid example and evidence of this is provided by the Petrograd Metalworkers' Union, which had only 70,000 members at the beginning of negotiations and over 180,000 after they ended.

After an exchange of opinions, the following resolution was accepted:

> The oblast conference of metalworkers of Moscow Industrial Region finds it necessary to raise a campaign by trade unions for wage rates agreements in the provinces. Unions' implementation of wage rates agreements should be guided by the following principles:
>
> 1. Unions should conclude wage rates agreements not case by case with individual enterprises, but collectively with societies of factory owners, syndicates, and similar associations.
>
> 2. Oblast unions' leadership should organize the wage rates campaign rather than conducting it separately by individual organizations.
>
> 3. Unions should establish a minimum wage during their implementation of wage rates agreements.
>
> 4. When wage rates agreements are established, priority should go to raising the wages of lowly paid categories of workers (the unskilled, women, and adolescents), according to the minimum necessary for subsistence.
>
> 5. In wage rates agreements, set wage rates should be raised systematically according to the growth of the cost of living.

The wage rates agreement campaign, when implemented on a broad scale, helps to organize worker masses into unions and to systematize economic struggle. Along with that, it raises wages in backward areas of production to the level of those in leading industrial centers. By improving workers' present economic situation, introducing wage uniformity for different localities, and doing away with isolated, unorganized acts, the wage rates agreement helps unite and economize the proletariat's forces. Given the country's current circumstances of world war, economic collapse, and untidy financial housekeeping, the conference finds it necessary to state that the wage rates agreement cannot extricate the working class from the difficult situation and deprivations, which were created by the high cost of living. It is only a palliative measure, which temporarily alleviates the acute disparity between wages and prices for consumer items.

Only radical change of all economic and financial policy in the direction toward regulating all of the country's economic life will make the goals of the wage rates agreement achievable. . . .[99]

* * *

The conclusion of a wage rates agreement was a major accomplishment during Russia's economic crisis in 1917. Yet the inability of a wage rates agreement to address fundamental inequities in the relationship between workers and owners encouraged Bolshevik trade union leaders' revolutionary impulses in the fall of 1917. The Petrograd Metalworkers' Union gave its support and 50,000 rubles from its treasury to help achieve the objective of Soviet power in October 1917.

PART V
The Bolsheviks' Post-Revolutionary Agenda for Workers

After the Bolsheviks came to power, Alexander Shlyapnikov joined the new revolutionary government as People's Commissar of Labor. He relied upon trade unions to provide staff for government bodies, to provide input into government policy-making, and to help implement government policy. The Commissariat of Labor undertook important and difficult tasks such as extending wage rates agreements to industry on a national scale, carrying out a program to nationalize industry, and elaborating a plan for workers' control, in which Shlyapnikov promoted unions over factory committees as the preferable method to organize workers. The Labor Commissariat's projects met with limited success. The wage rates agreement that was reached was published as a decree, but inflation rendered its rates useless. Ambitions for the unions' role in the workers' control project clashed with Lenin's political stake in the factory committees, which were far more pro-Bolshevik than were the unions in late 1917 and early 1918. Nationalization of enterprises foundered at a time of economic crisis. Shlyapnikov's appeal below, which was published in the newspaper Izvestia of the Soviet of Workers' and Soldiers' Deputies, reflects the stark challenges the new Bolshevik-dominated government saw to consolidating its power and that faced the Labor Commissariat as it attempted to enlist workers' energies in projects of economic revival and building socialism.

Alexander Shlyapnikov, "To All Workers"

December 22, 1917

From the People's Commissar of Labor to all Working Men, Working Women, and Office Personnel.

Comrades!

A time of unprecedented severity is approaching. Our country's industry, which was mobilized unsystematically during three and a half years of war and guided exclusively by the thirst for wartime profits, has been deprived of a significant share of [resources]. Reduction of war production occurs at a time when two classes and two worlds are engaged in the greatest struggle. One is the world of capitalist exploitation and oppression and the other is the world of fraternal cooperation by all those who are enslaved. Awful economic collapse accompanies political struggle between capital and labor across the entire country. Organizers of the capitalist economy—factory and mill owners, bankers, along with their lackey-collaborators (bureaucrats, engineers, and others who feed on the crumbs of profits)—attempt to make use of the approaching crisis to crush the revolution. With the skeletal hands of hunger and economic collapse, they are hanging the fatal noose around the neck of the working class.

Workers, soldiers, and peasants, who are all children of the revolution, should close ranks at this threatening hour. With their consciousness, unrestrained know-how, strong hands, and mighty shoulders, they should hold back our economy from collapse. Enterprises and worker organizations, which have been emancipated from military work, should adapt to producing consumer items. Each one should remember now that he no longer works for the sake of capitalists' profits. All laborers should remember that workers and peasants have become the actual masters of our country. Everyone should regard the mills, factories, other enterprises, and their work from the concerned standpoint of a good, disinterested socialist master.

Reduction of military orders, severe economic collapse leading to factory stoppages, the waste of worker intellect, the specter of hunger, and fear of unemployment hover over the heads of the broad, laboring masses. This fear, which we inherited from our fathers who were slaves, holds our cheerful thoughts in capitalist captivity, presents great obstacles toward emancipating all of humanity from the yoke of exploitation, and subjugates the masses with worries about tomorrow. Many rush to secure themselves from coming dangers by accumulating extra paper rubles. They demand new wage increases, pay for months ahead, or back pay upon finishing work, and so forth. The bourgeois press, provocateurs, and reactionary elements create theories of the "infinite increase of wages." They try to play upon this chasing after rubles and in doing so to create disorganization and schism within the working class.

Extra rubles will not help. Each working man and woman and each peasant man and woman should understand and remember that rubles will be cheaper if everyone has more of them. They will be dearer when there is less paper money and more goods. Therefore, all the efforts of the laboring masses should be directed toward organizing work and setting right our economy.

The government and the Coalition Ministries left complete economic collapse for revolutionary people. There is little bread, little metal, little clothing and underwear, and few shoes in the country. There is no firewood, no coal, no oil, and no kerosene. However, our country is rich with all these things. Like Sleeping Beauty, this wealth awaits the mighty touch of a laboring hand. Workers should not await their deliverance from the coming ordeal from above, nor should they reconcile themselves to relying upon more paper rubles, but they should build labor columns to extract metals, coal, firewood, and the like. Worker organizations such as trade unions and factory committees should organize work in collaboration with all technical personnel and even owners, if such are to be found. They should all unite in accord with an enormous economic system, which rests upon the independence of worker masses, who support strict labor discipline. Workers should regard with deep trust their fortress-organizations, not only as the demanding side. All demands now are addressed to themselves. If the working class will be able to organize production, distribution, exchange, railways, and factories, it will by this fulfill all its demands. If it will not—there awaits us a return to the past and to the yoke of exploitation, with all its sorrows and pain. The tasks of the working class are complex and responsible and great are its goals. In realization of their ideals, the laboring masses should exert all their efforts in conscious, organized work. The enemies of the working class, who are armed with experience and knowledge that they obtained on the people's money, await the downfall of the revolution and the failure of our tasks and work. We will close together in concerted ranks, under our organizations' red banners. With concerted, powerful efforts, we will conquer all obstacles that history has placed on our hard, laborers' road.[100]

CONCLUSION

The realities of holding power contrasted sharply with the emancipatory dreams of 1917. In the early months of Soviet rule, as counterrevolutionary armies formed and German troops surged into Russian territory, the Bolsheviks faced a fierce fight for the survival of their regime. Rapidly issuing decrees to mollify diverse leftist constituencies, they acquiesced to peasants seizing large estates, proclaimed workers' control of factories, nationalized banks, transport, and communications, and began peace negotiations. While organizing a government and army, they also aspired to craft a socialist society. Despite their increase in membership over the course of 1917, they were still a small urban party with no control over large swathes of the collapsing empire. To cope with developing crises and multiple agendas, the Bolsheviks often occupied multiple party, state, and military posts and carried out divergent assignments in various parts of the country, shifting rapidly from one work assignment or geographic area to another. The threat of counterrevolution overshadowed the Bolsheviks' new political, social, and economic experiment, making their struggle more desperate.

The question of maintaining power confronted the Bolsheviks as soon as they had wrested control from the Provisional Government. Party moderates, led by Grigory Zinoviev and Lev Kamenev, believed that the Bolsheviks were too weak to stay in power alone and favored a coalition government including representatives of other socialist parties. On November 3, 1917, the Soviet's Central Executive Committee voted in favor of Kamenev's and Zinoviev's resolution to bring other socialist parties into the government.

Lenin reacted furiously, threatening to "expel" the opposition from the party. In response, most moderates resigned from their CC and government posts. The subsequent inclusion of the Left SRs in the government appeased many of the moderates, however.[101]

Soon after the Bolsheviks took power, they pursued initiatives to weaken their opponents and consolidate their hold on power. On November 28, 1917, the Council of People's Commissars (Sovnarkom) approved Lenin's proposal to arrest liberal Constitutional Democratic (Kadet) party leaders and directed that they be turned over to a revolutionary court. The Kadet party was disbanded.[102] The Cheka, the Soviet secret police body led by Felix Dzerzhinsky, was founded to combat currency speculation, sabotage, and counterrevolution. The Bolshevik CC held the line that elections conducted for the Constituent Assembly in early October 1917 did not reflect the views of the masses by the time the Constituent Assembly convened in January 1918. Bolsheviks perceived the assembly as the "bourgeoisie's" last hope of creating a conservative government to preserve private property and determined not to allow it to function.[103]

As civil war began, the Red Guard's role developed on an ad hoc basis before it disappeared entirely. Red Guard units defended the Bolshevik hold on power from the very first days, when they helped defeat counterrevolutionary forces in the Battle of Pulkovo Heights near Petrograd.[104] Red Guards participated in the arrest of Kadet leaders, served as an instrument for enforcement of Cheka operations, and with "striking brutality" helped suppress demonstrations in favor of the Constituent Assembly.[105] In the early months of the Russian Civil War, Red Guard units from Moscow, Petrograd, and the Central Industrial Region went to the Don, Kiev, Kharkov, Mogilev, and Finland to fight counterrevolutionary forces.[106] As the Red Army formed, its nucleus included Red Guard leaders, but it was organized more like a regular military than in the style of a militia.[107] Still, workers preferred serving in irregular militias to longer terms of more disciplined duty in the Red Army, so voluntary recruitment to the latter went slowly. Conscription into the army was introduced in summer 1918.[108] When the Red Army was formed, there was no corresponding order to disperse militias like the Red Guards.

Nevertheless, they faded out of existence in the spring of 1918 in Petrograd and in Moscow in summer 1918 but survived in the Far East and Turkestan into 1919.[109] Among their last duties in European Russia were the defense of Moscow and of the German embassy in July 1918, and the requisition of food supplies in the rural areas.[110] Ideological enthusiasm for decentralized Red Guards and militias as revolutionary forces faded by 1921.[111]

The Bolsheviks struggled to establish a government of an entirely new type while their enemies mobilized against them and the economy collapsed around them. In the unpredictable and rapidly evolving context, the Commissariat of Labor (Narkomtrud) appropriated a broad role. Rather than simply mediating between workers and management (as the Provisional Government's Ministry of Labor had done), Narkomtrud aimed to promote workers' welfare and collaborate with trade unions to organize and regulate industry. Trade unions' work was crucial to the foundation of socialism. Key Narkomtrud positions were filled with trade union staff, whose expertise in the regulation of wages and working conditions seemed to qualify them to perform these duties in the government. Nevertheless, Narkomtrud faced tremendous challenges: the ambitions of the factory committees, the workers' interpretations of the state's responsibilities toward them, the need to ensure labor discipline, and the intransigent leaders of non-Bolshevik unions. Narkomtrud used its power to increase trade unions' role in economic management and government. Attempts to give economic power to the unions may have contributed to undermining their independence and their ability to defend workers.

The economic power of the unions was closely tied to Bolshevik decisions on how to hold on to political power. The metalworkers', textile workers' and leather workers' unions (all controlled by Bolsheviks) contributed the most staff to Narkomtrud and had representatives in the commissariat's board (collegium). The Mensheviks still controlled the All-Russian Central Council of Trade Unions (VTsSPS) in late 1917. Narkomtrud encouraged trade unionists to enter into other commissariats and government bodies, for example the All-Russian Council of National Economy (VSNKh). In its first several months of existence, VSNKh was run by Left Communists like Valerian Obolensky (N. Osinsky), who favored worker administration of factories, but when the Left Communists resigned from government in March 1918, VSNKh (under Lenin's direction) revised its stance to advocate appointed factory boards supervised by workers' organizations.[112]

In January 1918, at the First Trade Union Congress, the debate over trade union participation in government flared up dramatically. Menshevik delegates regarded the introduction of trade unionists into state institutions as syndicalist. The congress declared "organizing production" to be one of the unions' major tasks but seems to have left unresolved the exact relationship of the unions to government economic bodies. Nevertheless, as E. H. Carr wrote, the congress "virtually settled the principle of the subordination of the trade unions to the state, which now remained uncontested...for nearly three years."[113] Lack of clarity in the congress's decisions probably reflected dissension among Bolsheviks, some of whom sided with Mensheviks on trade union independence from government, such as David Ryazanov, who had played a leading role in organizing trade unions in St. Petersburg in 1905 and after the 1917 revolutions.[114] Other Bolsheviks saw no need for unions under a socialist regime. Questions about the role of the unions in the transition to socialism would simmer until the trade union debate of 1920–21.

Many of the questions Narkomtrud decided on in its first months of existence were related: the wage rates agreement, workers' control over industry, the nationalization of enterprises, and worker productivity. Many Bolshevik trade unionists were deeply committed to organized workers' control of industry under centralized coordination. To them, the nationalization of industry would ease the implementation of workers' control. For workers' control to succeed, and for nationalized industry not to bankrupt the state, labor productivity had to be guaranteed. Of all the projects on Narkomtrud's agenda, the wage rates agreement was perhaps the easiest to negotiate but one of the more difficult to implement. Faced with the factory owners' obstinate disinterest in working out a new agreement, Narkomtrud simply revised existing wage rates to account for inflation and published them as a decree. Its leaders hoped to attract workers from small industry to large nationalized enterprises, thus concentrating labor and resources in large enterprises and raising production to a higher level.[115] Nevertheless, rapid inflation made the wage rates agreement impractical and Narkomtrud was unable to enforce the agreement under conditions of economic collapse and the flight of both capital and capitalists.

The deteriorating economy and conflicting political priorities undermined other Narkomtrud projects, such as the first decree on workers' control. Crucial differences on workers' control existed among Bolsheviks and their organizations. Radical Bolsheviks aligned with the factory committees, and moderate socialists in trade unions disagreed on workers' control. Lenin perceived a danger that the moderate Bolsheviks would join forces with other moderate socialists in trade unions. He tried to undermine them by throwing his support to the radicals so his draft decree on workers' control reflected the wishes of factory-committee activists. The Narkomtrud draft decree reflected the views of moderate Bolshevik trade unionists.[116]

Lenin envisioned only including representatives of the soviets and factory committees in economic regulatory institutions, but Narkomtrud placed equal emphasis on the role of the trade unions. In Lenin's draft, factory committees would supervise the day-to-day work of the factory, while trade unions would merely serve as higher institutions of appeal. Narkomtrud's draft assigned the formulation of regulations to councils of workers' control, with only an executive role for the factory committee. Another key difference was that Narkomtrud allowed participation in workers' control by workers who held various political views, while Lenin's draft was designed to ensure that his confederates would dominate.

Although the final decree incorporated most of Narkomtrud's proposals and was confirmed by Sovnarkom and endorsed by the soviets, Lenin conspired with factory-committee leaders to circumvent it. With Lenin's encouragement, in practice the factory committees ignored the soviets' legislation. Thus the Central Council of Workers' Control (composed of Petrograd Trade Union Council members) had no real power and was supplanted by VSNKh. Lenin, however, soon abandoned the factory committees. By March 1918, the Bolsheviks had largely captured the trade unions from the Mensheviks, so the factory committees were no longer of use. Lenin readily agreed to the factory committees being subordinated to the trade unions.[117]

The Bolsheviks had nothing more than a vague commitment to nationalizing industry when they came to power. Narkomtrud leaders hoped that the nationalization of industry would facilitate the centralized coordination of workers' control of industry, halt Russia's economic collapse, and rationalize the economy to make it stronger and more productive. Banks and important industrial sectors, such as oil, coal, sugar, metallurgy, and transport, would be nationalized. However, no plan existed for how to accomplish nationalization, or how quickly. Narkomtrud played a crucial role in recommending which factories to nationalize. One of the challenges included convincing workers to turn profits over to the state. Sometimes mistakes were made when enterprises that turned out to be unprofitable were too hastily nationalized. Consequently, Narkomtrud appointed commissions to determine the profitability of enterprises before nationalizing them.[118]

The decline of industry threatened to derail plans for workers' control and the nationalization of industry. One of the first steps in limiting workers' responsibility for the economy was when the government reintroduced one-man management for railways on March 26, 1918, replacing colleges (boards) composed of two or more men, including union representatives. Railway unions could still send representatives to sit on commissariat boards, but their candidates had to be confirmed by Sovnarkom and VTsSPS. Since socialists who opposed the Bolshevik government controlled the All-Russian Executive Committee of Railwaymen [Vikzhel], which had pressured the Bolsheviks to form a coalition government after their seizure of power, some Bolshevik leaders accepted coercion against them.[119] Politics created some inconsistencies in Bolshevik trade unionists' commitment to union power.

Government and union leaders hoped to help reverse economic decline by requiring workers to guarantee that they would turn out products.[120] Guarantees of productivity had been contentious before the revolution and continued to be so. The chief question was enforcement. Some officials called for tighter discipline and harsher punishments, including dismissal, to encourage workers to work harder. Others insisted that weakness from hunger, rather than lack of discipline, was to blame for the decline in productivity. The solution, they insisted, lay in "higher wages, greater workers' control and moral suasion." Some called controversially for the revival of piece rates,[121] as an incentive for workers to work harder. Piece rates had largely been abolished after the February Revolution and had not returned since then, even though unions had allowed for them in their 1917 wage rates agreements. The Petrograd Metalworkers' Union was in favor of piece rates, but the Petrograd Council of Trade Unions was not. Ryazanov, an influential member of the council, deemed piece rates an exploitative practice that was "incompatible with socialism." Practices such as piece rates and Taylorism, however, were compatible with the views of some prominent members of the Metalworkers' Union, who composed the "Platform of Labor Industrialism" group in early 1918. They imagined that socialist production would not only ensure a comfortable life for workers but would also create a culture of labor and foster innovation. They were thus open to some capitalist methods designed to encourage innovation. In the 1917 wage rates agreement between the Metalworkers' Union and factory owners, piece-work pay had not been intended to replace wages designated by agreement, but to supplement them, accounting for no more than 25 percent of pay beyond normal wages.[122] The survival of industry and of the industrial working class hinged on productivity, and its advocates tried to justify the revival of piece rates and a guarantee of productivity by arguing that workers' control would ensure that exploitation would not occur. Indisputably, however, piece rates were a means of squeezing surplus value from workers.

To prevent workers from abandoning industry for other professions and trades, Narkomtrud leaders requested that Sovnarkom issue to Narkomtrud 30 million rubles to fund cafeterias, rations, and work projects for the unemployed. They also asked Sovnarkom to issue 500,000 rubles to fund trade unions, insurance committees, and other workers' organizations, as well as to publish works on "questions of workers' politics."[123] Sovnarkom refused both requests from Narkomtrud, but at the same meeting granted aid to a provincial bureaucrats' union.[124] To some in Narkomtrud and in industrial trade unions, this may have been an ominous harbinger of the priority the Bolsheviks, who renamed themselves the Russian Communist Party (Bolshevik) in March 1918, would place on coercion toward workers and bureaucratic centralization of government economic bodies as a means to support the waging of the coming civil war.

By the time the Communists achieved victory in 1920–21, some of those workers who had been on the forefront of revolutionary organizing in 1917 perceived that the Communists had departed from the original goals of the October Revolution to give workers power to direct their own destinies. Some of them would gather in the Workers' Opposition to advocate trade union management of the economy and to call for workers to take back the reins in the party and the soviets.

BIBLIOGRAPHY

Archives

Rossiiskii gosudarstvennyi arkhiv sotsialno-politicheskoi istorii (RGASPI) –
Russian State Archive of Social and Political History
———. Fond 17 CPSU Central Committee, 1898, 1903-91
———. Fond 19 Protocols of Sovnarkom, Little Sovnarkom, and RSFSR
Council of Labor and Defense, 1917-22
———. Fond 70 Commission on the History of the October Revolution and of
the Russian Communist Party (Bolshevik), 1920–28
Gosudarstvennyi arkhiv Rossiiskoi Federatsii (GARF) – State Archive of the
Russian Federation
———. Fond 130 Council of People's Commissars
———. Fond 382 Commissariat of Labor (Narkomtrud)
———. Fond 5469 All-Russian Metalworkers' Union Central Committee

Periodicals

Izvestia, daily of the Petrograd Soviet of Workers' and Soldiers' Deputies
Metallist, bimonthly of the All-Russian and Petrograd Metalworkers' Unions
Pravda, daily of the Russian Social Democratic Workers' Party (Bolshevik)
Rabochaia gazeta, daily of the Russian Social Democratic Workers' Party (Menshevik)

Books and Articles

Allen, Barbara C. *Alexander Shlyapnikov, 1885–1937: Life of an Old Bolshevik.*
Leiden, The Netherlands: Brill, 2015.
Anonymous. "About the Red Guard." *Rabochaia gazeta*, no. 43 (April 29, 1917): 1–2.
———. "Editorial." *Rabochaia gazeta*, no. 43 (April 29, 1917).
———. "Iz zhizni soiuza." *Metallist*, nos. 1–2 (August 17, 1917): 19–23.
———. "Konflikty metallistov." *Metallist*, nos. 1–2 (August 17, 1917): 15.
Ansky, A., ed. *Professionalnoe dvizhenie v Petrograde v 1917 g.* Leningrad: Len. Obl.
Prof. Sov., 1928.

Bailes, Kendall E. "Alexei Gastev and the Soviet Controversy over Taylorism, 1918–24." *Soviet Studies*, 29, no. 3 (1977): 373–94.

Beecher, Jonathan, and Valerii N. Fomichev. "French Socialism in Lenin's and Stalin's Moscow: David Ryazanov and the French Archive of the Marx-Engels Institute." *Journal of Modern History* 78, no. 1 (2006): 119–43.

Bonnell, Victoria, ed. *The Russian Worker: Life and Labor under the Tsarist Regime.* Berkeley: University of California Press, 1983.

Brovkin, Vladimir, ed. "Workers' Unrest and the Bolsheviks' Response in 1919." *Slavic Review* 49, no. 3 (1991): 350–73.

Bulkin, F. *Soiuz metallistov, 1906–1918 gg.: kratkii istoricheskii ocherk.* Moscow, 1926.

Burdzhalov, Eduard N. *Russia's Second Revolution: The February 1917 Uprising in Petrograd.* Translated and edited by Donald J. Raleigh. Bloomington: Indiana University Press, 1987.

Carr, Edward Hallett. *The Bolshevik Revolution, 1917–1923.* 3 volumes. London: Macmillan, 1950–53.

Fitzpatrick, Sheila. *The Russian Revolution.* Oxford: Oxford University Press, 2017.

Flenley, Paul. "Industrial Relations and the Economic Crisis of 1917." *Revolutionary Russia* 4, no. 2 (1991): 184–209.

Gambarov, Iu. et al., eds. *Deiateli SSSR i oktiabr'skoi revoliutsii: avtobiografii i biografii.* 3 vols. Moscow: Granat, 1927–29. Reprint, Moscow: Kniga, 1989.

Gastev, Aleksey. "Obrashchenie vsem rabochim-metallistam Rossii." *Metallist*, nos. 1–2 (1917): 24.

Georgievsky, R. P. *Ocherki po istorii krasnoi gvardii.* Moscow: Fakel, 1919.

Goltsman, Abram. "Pervyi god." *Metallist*, nos. 3–4 (July 15, 1918): 3.

———. "Kak byl sozdan vserossiiskii soiuz rabochikh-metallistov." *Metallist* 1917–1927, anniversary issue, pp. 64–66.

Gruber, Helmut, ed. *International Communism in the Era of Lenin: A Documentary History.* Ithaca, NY: Cornell University Press, 1967.

Hasegawa, Tsuyoshi. *The February Revolution: Petrograd, 1917.* Seattle: University of Washington Press, 1981.

Hickey, Michael C. *Competing Voices from the Russian Revolution: Fighting Words.* Santa Barbara, CA: Greenwood, 2010.

Lepse, Ivan. "Petrogradskii soiuz rabochikh-metallistov v 1917 godu." *Metallist* 1917–1927 (anniversary issue), 69–72.

Lih, Lars T. "The Ironic Triumph of Old Bolshevism: The Debates of April 1917 in Context." *Russian History* 38, no. 2 (2011): 199–242.

Longley, D. A. "The Divisions in the Bolshevik Party in March 1917." *Soviet Studies* 24, no. 1 (1972): 61–76.

———. "The Mezhraionka, the Bolsheviks, and International Women's Day: In Response to Michael Melancon." *Soviet Studies* 41, no. 4 (1989): 625–45.

Malakhovsky, V. I. "Kak sozdavalas rabochaia krasnaia gvardiia." *Proletarskaia revoliutsiia*, no. 10 (1929): 27–79.

Mawdsley, Evan. *The Russian Revolution and the Baltic Fleet: War and Politics, February 1917–April 1918.* London: Macmillan, 1978.

Melancon, Michael. *From the Head of Zeus: The Petrograd Soviet's Rise and First Days, 27 February–2 March 1917.* The Carl Beck Papers in Russian and East European Studies. Pittsburgh: University of Pittsburgh/CREES, 2009.

————. "Who Wrote What and When: Proclamations of the February Revolution in Petrograd, 23 February–1 March 1917." *Soviet Studies* 40, no. 3 (1988): 479–500.

Naumov, V. P. *Aleksandr Gavrilovich Shliapnikov: stranitsy politicheskoi biografii, Novoe v zhizni, nauke, tekhnike: seriia politicheskaia istoriia XX veka,* no. 8. Moscow: Znanie, 1991.

Obolensky, V.V. (N. Osinsky). "Iz pervykh dnei VSNKh." *Narodnoe khoziaistvo,* no. 11 (1918): 11–14.

Oppenheim, Samuel A. "The Supreme Economic Council, 1917–1921." *Soviet Studies* 25, no. 1 (1973): 3–27.

Rabinowitch, Alexander. *The Bolsheviks Come to Power: The Revolution of 1917 in Petrograd.* New York: W. W. Norton, 1976.

————. *The Bolsheviks in Power: The First Year of Soviet Rule in Petrograd.* Bloomington: Indiana University Press, 2007.

————. *Prelude to Revolution: The Petrograd Bolsheviks and the July 1917 Uprising.* Bloomington: Indiana University Press, 1991.

Schapiro, Leonard. *The Origin of the Communist Autocracy: Political Opposition in the Soviet State, First Phase, 1917–1922.* Cambridge, MA: Harvard University Press, 1956.

Service, Robert. *Lenin: A Political Life.* 3 vols. Bloomington: Indiana University Press, 1991.

Shkliarevsky, Gennady. *Labor in the Russian Revolution: Factory Committees and Trade Unions, 1917–1918.* New York: St. Martin's Press, 1993.

Shlyapnikov, Alexander. "Borba za minimum zarabotnoi platy v metallicheskoi promyshlennosti v Pitere." *Pravda,* no. 93 (1917): 9.

————. "Eshche raz ob organizatsii soiuzov." *Metallist,* no. 5 (November 9, 1917): 2.

————. *Kanun semnadtsatogo goda.* 2 vols. Moscow/Petrograd: Gosizdat, 1923.

————. *Kanun semnadtsatogo goda; Semnadtsatyi god.* 3 vols. 1923–31. Commentary and preface by A. S. Smolnikov and A. A. Chernobaev. Reprint, Moscow: Politizdat, 1992.

————. "K oktiabriu." *Proletarskaia revoliutsiia,* no. 10 (1922): 11–12.

————. "Nash tarif." *Metallist,* nos. 1–2 (August 17, 1917): 3–6.

————. "Novyi tarif rabochikh-metallistov." *Metallist,* no. 2 (1918): 14.

————. "O konferentsii soiuza rabochikh-metallistov Moskovskoi oblasti." *Metallist,* no. 5 (November 9, 1917): 11.

————. "Pamiati 'uchredilki.'" *Ogonek* 5, no. 44 (1924): 9–10.

————. *Semnadtsatyi god.* 4 vols. Moscow/Petrograd: Gosizdat, 1923–31.

————. "U nas dolzhen byt tolko odin soiuz rabochikh-metallistov." *Metallist,* nos. 1–2 (August 17, 1917): 13–14.

————. "V.I. Lenin i Narkomtrud (po lichnym vospominaniiam)," *Voprosy truda,* 3 (1924): 3–5.

————. "Zadachi rastsenochnykh komissii." *Metallist,* no. 3 (October 1, 1917): 3–4.

Shlyapnikov, Alexander (pseud. A. Belenin). "O 'krasnoi gvardii.'" *Pravda,* no. 49 (May 5, 1917): 5.

Smele, Jonathan D. *The "Russian" Civil Wars, 1916–1926: Ten Years That Shook the World.* Oxford: Oxford University Press, 2017.

Smith, Stephen A. *Red Petrograd: Revolution in the Factories, 1917–1918.* Cambridge: Cambridge University Press, 1983.

————. *Russia in Revolution: An Empire in Crisis, 1890 to 1928.* Oxford: Oxford University Press, 2017.

Sorenson, Jay. *The Life and Death of Soviet Trade Unionism: 1917–1928.* New York: Atherton Press, 1969.

Thatcher, Ian D. "The St. Petersburg/Petrograd Mezhraionka, 1913–1917: The Rise and Fall of a Russian Social Democratic Workers' Party Unity Faction." *Slavonic and East European Review* 87, no. 2 (2009): 284–321.

Thompson, John M. *Revolutionary Russia, 1917.* New York: Scribner, 1981.

Wade, Rex A. *Red Guards and Workers' Militias in the Russian Revolution.* Stanford, CA: Stanford University Press, 1984.

————. *The Russian Revolution, 1917.* Cambridge: Cambridge University Press, 2000.

White, James D. "The February Revolution and the Bolshevik Vyborg District Committee (in Response to Michael Melancon)." *Soviet Studies* 41, no. 4 (1989): 602–24.

Zelnik, Reginald. *Law and Disorder on the Narova River: The Kreenholm Strike of 1872.* Berkeley: University of California Press, 1995.

NOTES

1   Other recent collections of translated documents from the Russian Revolution include Laurie Bernstein and Robert Weinberg, *Revolutionary Russia: A History in Documents* (New York: Oxford University Press, 2010); Jonathan Daly and Leonid Trofimov, eds. and trans., *Russia in War and Revolution, 1914–1922: A Documentary History* (Indianapolis: Hackett, 2009); Jonathan Daly and Leonid Trofimov, eds., *The Russian Revolution and Its Global Impact: A Short History with Documents* (Indianapolis: Hackett, 2017); Michael C. Hickey, ed. and trans., *Competing Voices from the Russian Revolution: Fighting Words* (Santa Barbara, CA: Greenwood, 2010); and Mark D. Steinberg, *Voices of the Revolution, 1917*, trans. Marian C. Schwartz (New Haven, CT: Yale University Press, 2002).

2   Barbara C. Allen, *Alexander Shlyapnikov, 1885–1937: Life of an Old Bolshevik* (Leiden, The Netherlands: Brill, 2015; Chicago: Haymarket Books, 2016).

3   Rex A. Wade, *The Russian Revolution, 1917* (Cambridge: Cambridge University Press, 2000), 29–36; Tsuyoshi Hasegawa, *The February Revolution: Petrograd, 1917* (Seattle: University of Washington Press, 1981), 278–94; Eduard N. Burdzhalov, *Russia's Second Revolution: The February 1917 Uprising in Petrograd*, trans. and ed. Donald J. Raleigh (Bloomington: Indiana University Press, 1987), 102; John M. Thompson, *Revolutionary Russia, 1917* (New York: Scribner, 1981), 21.

4   Michael Melancon, "Who Wrote What and When: Proclamations of the February Revolution in Petrograd, 23 February–1 March 1917," *Soviet Studies* 40, no. 3 (1988): 479–500; Michael Melancon, *From the Head of Zeus: The Petrograd Soviet's Rise and First Days, 27 February–2 March 1917*, The Carl Beck Papers in Russian and East European Studies (Pittsburgh: University of Pittsburgh/ CREES, 2009); Wade, *Russian Revolution, 1917*, 34–35; Burdzhalov, *Russia's Second Revolution*, 86, 180; Alexander Shlyapnikov, *Kanun semnadtsatogo goda; Semnadtsatyi god*, vol. 2 of 3, commentary and preface by A. S. Smolnikov and A. A. Chernobaev (Moscow: Politizdat, [1925] 1992), 62–65, 91–95; Hasegawa, *February Revolution*, 296.

5   Hasegawa, *February Revolution*, 334–42, 356–57; Shlyapnikov, *Kanun semnadtsatogo goda; Semnadtsatyi god*, 2:26–132; Rossiiskii gosudarstvennyi arkhiv sotsialno-politicheskoi istorii (RGASPI), f. 70, op. 4, d. 387, l. 132; Wade,

Russian Revolution, 1917, 91, 94. The Executive Committee was identical to an all-socialist group that had met in the weeks before the February Revolution (Melancon, *From the Head of Zeus*).

6 Wade, *Russian Revolution, 1917,* 53–58.

7 The differences among the Bolsheviks are discussed in detail by Alexander Rabinowitch, *Prelude to Revolution: The Petrograd Bolsheviks and the July 1917 Uprising* (Bloomington: Indiana University Press, 1991), 33–35; and D. A. Longley, "The Divisions in the Bolshevik Party in March 1917," *Soviet Studies* 24, no. 1 (1972): 67. For a different reading of these events, see Lars T. Lih, "The Ironic Triumph of Old Bolshevism: The Debates of April 1917 in Context," *Russian History* 38, no. 2 (2011): 199–242.

8 Shlyapnikov, *Kanun semnadtsatogo goda*; *Semnadtsatyi god,* 2:65–66, 163–165; Longley, "Divisions in the Bolshevik Party," 67; Leonard Schapiro, *The Origin of the Communist Autocracy: Political Opposition in the Soviet State, First Phase, 1917–1922* (Cambridge, MA: Harvard University Press, 1956), 28; and V. P. Naumov, *Aleksandr Gavrilovich Shliapnikov: stranitsy politicheskoi biografii, Novoe v zhizni, nauke, tekhnike: seriia politicheskaia istoriia XX veka,* no. 8 (Moscow: Znanie, 1991), 16.

9 Shlyapnikov, *Kanun semnadtsatogo goda*; *Semnadtsatyi god,* 2:445–48.

10 Longley, "The Divisions in the Bolshevik Party in March 1917," 66, 72; Shlyapnikov, *Kanun semnadtsatogo goda*; *Semnadtsatyi god,* 2:439, 452; Rabinowitch, *Prelude to Revolution,* 36.

11 Robert Service, *Lenin: A Political Life,* vol. 2., *Worlds in Collision* (Bloomington: Indiana University Press, 1991), 145–46; Rabinowitch, *Prelude to Revolution,* 36–45. The train was "sealed" in that German officials agreed not to enter (Wade, *Russian Revolution, 1917,* 73).

12 Rabinowitch, *Prelude to Revolution,* 40–46.

13 Shlyapnikov, *Kanun semnadtsatogo goda*; *Semnadtsatyi god,* 2:132; Rex A. Wade, *Red Guards and Workers' Militias in the Russian Revolution* (Stanford, CA: Stanford University Press, 1984), 43–44.

14 Wade, *Red Guards and Workers' Militias,* 61; Shlyapnikov, *Kanun semnadtsatogo goda*; *Semnadtsatyi god,* 2:389–91.

15 Shlyapnikov, *Kanun semnadtsatogo goda*; *Semnadtsatyi god,* 2:392–93; RGASPI, f. 70, op. 4, d. 387, l. 132; Wade, *Red Guards and Workers' Militias,* 97; R. P. Georgievsky, *Ocherki po istorii krasnoi gvardii* (Moscow: Fakel, 1919), 66–67.

16 Anonymous, "Editorial," *Rabochaia gazeta,* 43 (1917); Alexander Shlyapnikov (pseud. A. Belenin), "O 'krasnoi gvardii'," *Pravda,* no. 49 (1917): 5. V. I. Malakhovsky claimed that the Red Guard was revolutionary from the start ("Kak sozdavalas rabochaia krasnaia gvardiia," *Proletarskaia revoliutsiia,* no. 10 [1929]: 5). In an unpublished article, Shlyapnikov attacked Malakhovsky's claim, which in his opinion contradicted the party's actual goal of power

through the soviets and through mass struggle (RGASPI, f. 70, op. 3, d. 896, ll. 5–6, '*Otvet eshche odnomu fal'sifikatoru istorii*').

17 Stephen A. Smith, *Red Petrograd: Revolution in the Factories, 1917–1918* (Cambridge: Cambridge University Press, 1983), 104–5; Ivan Lepse, "Petrogradskii soiuz rabochikh-metallistov v 1917 godu," *Metallist 1917–1927* (anniversary issue), 69.

18 Anonymous, "Iz zhizni soiuza," *Metallist*, nos. 1–2 (August 17, 1917): 19–22; Kendall E. Bailes, "Alexei Gastev and the Soviet Controversy over Taylorism, 1918–24," *Soviet Studies*, no. 29 (1977): 385; Gosudarstvennyi arkhiv Rossiiskoi Federatsii (GARF), f. 5469, op. 1, d. 33, l. 1, Metalworkers' Union board meeting, May 27, 1917. The union central committee included five representatives of each city district, elected by district assemblies. Volkov may have been arrested in a Bolshevik repressive action against the Mensheviks in July 1918. See Vladimir Brovkin, ed., "Workers' Unrest and the Bolsheviks' Response in 1919," *Slavic Review* 49, no. 3 (1991): 122.

19 The All-Russian Metalworkers' Union was formed simultaneously with the convocation of the Third All-Russian Conference of Trade Unions. The First All-Russian Conference of Trade Unions had been held in October 1905 and the second conference in late February 1906.

20 GARF, f. 5469, op. 1, d. 2, l. 4; F. Bulkin, *Soiuz metallistov, 1906–1918 gg.: kratkii istoricheskii ocherk* (Moscow, 1926), 180, 190.

21 GARF, f. 5469, op. 1, d. 4, ll. 1–4; d. 33, l. 1; A. K. Gastev, "Obrashchenie vsem rabochim-metallistam Rossii," *Metallist*, nos. 1–2 (August 17, 1917): 24; A. Goltsman, "Kak byl sozdan vserossiiskii soiuz rabochikh-metallistov," *Metallist 1917–1927* (anniversary issue), 66.

22 GARF, f. 5469, op. 1, d. 33, ll. 2–5; Gennady Shkliarevsky, *Labor in the Russian Revolution: Factory Committees and Trade Unions, 1917–1918* (New York: St. Martin's Press, 1993), 26–29.

23 Anonymous, "Iz zhizni soiuza," 20; Shkliarevsky, *Labor in the Russian Revolution*, xi–xiv.

24 Anonymous, "Konflikty metallistov," *Metallist*, nos. 1–2 (August 17, 1917): 15. The Russian term for wage rates table or agreement was *tarif*, which probably derived from the German word of the same spelling, meaning "rates." Reginald Zelnik, *Law and Disorder on the Narova River: The Kreenholm Strike of 1872* (Berkeley: University of California Press, 1995), 78n79. I use the term *wage rates* in this book to avoid confusion with the English word *tariff*, which can mean "tax" or "duty."

25 Smith, *Red Petrograd*, 119–21.

26 Alexander Shlyapnikov, "Nash tarif," *Metallist*, nos. 1–2 (August 17, 1917): 3; Gastev, "Obrashchenie vsem rabochim-metallistam Rossii," 67.

27 Shlyapnikov, "Nash tarif," 3–4; Anonymous, "Iz zhizni soiuza," 20; and Smith, *Red Petrograd*, 122.

28   Smith, *Red Petrograd*, 121–24.

29   Shlyapnikov, "Nash tarif," 4; Anonymous, "Iz zhizni soiuza," 20; Shlyapnikov, "Borba za minimum zarabotnoi platy v metallicheskoi promyshlennosti v Pitere," *Pravda*, no. 93 (1917): 9.

30   Shlyapnikov, "Nash tarif," 4; Anonymous, "Iz zhizni soiuza," 20; Smith, *Red Petrograd*, 125.

31   Wade, *Russian Revolution, 1917*, 172–80.

32   Rabinowitch, *Prelude to Revolution*, 135–214, and *The Bolsheviks Come to Power: The Revolution of 1917 in Petrograd* (New York: W. W. Norton, 1976): 32–34; Wade, *Russian Revolution, 1917*, 181–184. For the role of the Kronstadt sailors, see Evan Mawdsley, *The Russian Revolution and the Baltic Fleet: War and Politics, February 1917-April 1918* (London: Macmillan, 1978). Sources differ on whether the Bolshevik Military Organization or armed detachments of the "workers' guard" or "factory militia" led demonstrating workers on their way to the Tauride Palace on July 4. Since membership in worker militias seems to have dropped precipitously during spring 1917, it is unlikely that they or the Red Guard played a significant role in the July Uprising (Shlyapnikov, *Kanun semnadtsatogo goda*; *Semnadtsatyi god*, vol. 3 of 3 (Moscow: Politizdat, [1927] 1992), 621; Rabinowitch, *Prelude to Revolution*, 276n45). Another complicating factor is that some individuals, Kirill Orlov for one, belonged to both the Bolshevik Military Organization and the Red Guard.

33   Shlyapnikov, *Kanun semnadtsatogo goda*; *Semnadtsatyi god*, vol. 3, kn. 4: pp. 620, 650–56, 669.

34   Paul Flenley, "Industrial Relations and the Economic Crisis of 1917," *Revolutionary Russia* 4, no. 2 (1991): 184–209; Shlyapnikov, "Nash tarif," 4–5. Shlyapnikov's data on actual wages for unskilled workers came from his union's labor exchange.

35   Smith, *Red Petrograd*, 125–126; Anonymous, "Iz zhizni soiuza," 21.

36   Smith, *Red Petrograd*, 129; Shlyapnikov, "Nash tarif," 3, 6.

37   Victoria Bonnell, ed., *The Russian Worker: Life and Labor under the Tsarist Regime* (Berkeley: University of California Press, 1983), 231.

38   Alexander Shlyapnikov, "Eshche raz ob organizatsii soiuzov," *Metallist*, no. 5 (November 9, 1917), 2; Alexander Shlyapnikov, "U nas dolzhen byt tolko odin soiuz rabochikh-metallistov," *Metallist*, nos. 1–2 (August 17, 1917): 13–14. The unions of the stokers and welders only joined the Metalworkers' Union in 1918 (Smith, *Red Petrograd*, 106–7).

39   Smith, *Red Petrograd*, 107–9; Shkliarevsky, *Labor in the Russian Revolution*, 69.

40   Shlyapnikov, "O konferentsii soiuza rabochikh-metallistov Moskovskoi oblasti," *Metallist*, no. 5 (November 9, 1917): 11; Smith, *Red Petrograd*, 105. The higher number comes from A. Ansky, ed., *Professionalnoe dvizhenie v Petrograde v 1917 g.* (Leningrad: Len. Obl. Prof. Sov., 1928), and the lower number was an estimate by the Provisional Government's Ministry of Labor.

41 Shkliarevsky, *Labor in the Russian Revolution*, 71; Smith, *Red Petrograd*, 110–12. For a breakdown by district of each party's supporters, see Smith, *Red Petrograd*, 104–5, 113. For an elucidation of the complex political fluctuations in 1917, see Wade, *Russian Revolution, 1917*, especially chapter Three.

42 Abram Goltsman, "Pervyi god," *Metallist*, nos. 3–4 (July 15, 1918): 3; Shlyapnikov, "O konferentsii soiuza rabochikh-metallistov Moskovskoi oblasti," 10; GARF, f. 5469, op. 1, d. 4, ll. 28–29.

43 Wade, *Russian Revolution, 1917*, 194–205.

44 Wade, *Russian Revolution, 1917*, 140–49, 188.

45 Rabinowitch, *Bolsheviks Come to Power*, 170, 187.

46 Rabinowitch, *Bolsheviks Come to Power*, 193–96, 201–6; Alexander Shlyapnikov, "K oktiabriu," *Proletarskaia revoliutsiia*, no. 10 (1922): 11–12.

47 Rabinowitch, *Bolsheviks Come to Power*, 218–19, 221.

48 Shlyapnikov, "K oktiabriu," 21–22; RGASPI, f. 70, op. 4, d. 387, l. 134; Shkliarevsky, *Labor in the Russian Revolution*, 96–97.

49 Rabinowitch, *Bolsheviks Come to Power*, 222–306; Shlyapnikov, "K oktiabriu," 21–22; RGASPI, f. 70, op. 4, d. 387, l. 134; Shkliarevsky, *Labor in the Russian Revolution*, 96–97. The two proletarians were Alexander Shlyapnikov and Victor Nogin, both of whom had worked in Petersburg factories. The sailor Pavel Dybenko and the university-educated Alexey Rykov were from the peasantry.

50 "Manifesto of the Zimmerwald Left," in Helmut Gruber, ed., *International Communism in the Era of Lenin: A Documentary History* (Ithaca, NY: Cornell University Press, 1967), 62–66.

51 These are lines from the 1897 poem "Proshchanie" ("Farewell") by Peter Filippovich Iakubovich (1860–1911), a member of the People's Will who had graduated from St. Petersburg University with a major in history and philology.

52 Final lines of the poem "Semia, poklevannoe ptitsami" ("Seeds pecked up by birds") by the Silver Age Symbolist poet Ivan Sergeevich Rukavishnikov (1877–1930), who was a Socialist Revolutionary.

53 Appeal from the Organizing Committee of the SD (Social Democratic) fractions of Higher Educational Institutions, December 1916. Published in Alexander Shlyapnikov, *Kanun semnadtsatogo goda*, vol. 2 (Moscow/Petrograd: Gosizdat, 1923), 63–67.

54 Rabinowitch, *Prelude to Revolution*, 24–25.

55 For more on the Mezhraionka, see D. A. Longley, "The Mezhraionka, the Bolsheviks, and International Women's Day: In Response to Michael Melancon," *Soviet Studies* 41, no. 4 (1989): 625–45; Melancon, "Who Wrote What and When," 479–500; Ian D. Thatcher, "The St. Petersburg/Petrograd Mezhraionka, 1913–1917: The Rise and Fall of a Russian Social Democratic Workers' Party Unity Faction," *Slavonic and East European Review* 87, no. 2

(April 2009): 284–321; James D. White, "The February Revolution and the Bolshevik Vyborg District Committee (in Response to Michael Melancon)," *Soviet Studies* 41, no. 4 (1989): 602–24.

56 During the 1905 Revolution, Trepov served as governor general of St. Petersburg and assistant interior minister.

57 Prince Georgy Lvov was a leader of the zemstvo movement, which was committed to local self-government in the face of tsarist opposition, and would be the first head of the Provisional Government. Russian historian Pavel Milyukov was a liberal politician who led the Constitutional Democratic Party (Kadets). Alexander Guchkov was a leader of the conservative Octobrist Party. Both would serve the Provisional Government—Milyukov as foreign minister and Guchkov as minister of war.

58 Printed leaflet issued by the Petersburg Interdistrict Committee prior to January 9, 1917. Published in Alexander Shlyapnikov, *Semnadtsatyi god*, vol. 1 of 4 (Moscow/Petrograd: Gosizdat, 1923), 265–68.

59 This translation was not included in the series *1917: The View from the Streets* and is first published in this book.

60 Baron Boris Stürmer served in various high Russian imperial government posts in 1916.

61 Printed leaflet issued prior to January 9, 1917 by the Petersburg Initiative Group of Social Democrats (Mensheviks). Published in Alexander Shlyapnikov, *Semnadtsatyi god*, 1:264–65.

62 Published in Alexander Shlyapnikov, *Semnadtsatyi god*, 1:279–80.

63 Published in Alexander Shlyapnikov, *Semnadtsatyi god*, 1:303–6.

64 Yngvild Sørbye pointed out to me that the holiday initially had to be celebrated on a Sunday, which led to varying dates in March (March 19, 1911; March 3, 1912; March 8, 1914; March 7, 1915; and so on). See also www.internationalwomensday.com/About (last accessed August 19, 2017).

65 Hasegawa, *February Revolution*, 215–18; Allen, *Alexander Shlyapnikov, 1885–1937*.

66 Published in Russian in Alexander Shlyapnikov, *Semnadtsatyi god*, 1:1923, 306–8.

67 Hasegawa, *February Revolution*, 258–61; Stephen A. Smith, *Russia in Revolution: An Empire in Crisis, 1890 to 1928* (Oxford University Press, 2017), 101–2; Wade, *Russian Revolution, 1917*, 29–45.

68 Published in Russian in Alexander Shlyapnikov, *Semnadtsatyi god*, 1:337–38.

69 Melancon, *From the Head of Zeus*, 37–39, with long translated excerpts from the leaflet; Wade, *Russian Revolution, 1917*, 45–52, 101–2.

70 Published in Russian in Alexander Shlyapnikov, *Semnadtsatyi god*, 1:306–8.

71 Wade, *Russian Revolution, 1917*, 67–70. For a Bolshevik response to this policy, see John Riddell, "Mandate for Soviet Elections," johnriddell.wordpress.

com/2017/03/23/pravda-draft-mandate-for-soviet-elections, March 23, 2017.

72 First published in *Izvestia*, no. 15 (March 15, 1917). Reprinted in Alexander Shlyapnikov, *Semnadtsatyi god*, vol. 2 of 4 (Moscow/Petrograd: Gosizdat, 1925), 291.

73 Wade, *Russian Revolution, 1917*, 85–86.

74 Reprinted in Alexander Shlyapnikov, *Semnadtsatyi god*, vol. 4 of 4 (Moscow/Petrograd: Gosizdat, 1931), 25–26.

75 Reprinted in Alexander Shlyapnikov, *Semnadtsatyi god*, 4:26–28.

76 Rabinowitch, *Prelude to Revolution*, 54–79; Wade, *Russian Revolution, 1917*, 179–80.

77 Both documents reprinted in Alexander Shlyapnikov, *Semnadtsatyi god*, 4:404–6.

78 Rabinowitch, *Prelude to Revolution*, 54–79; Wade, *Russian Revolution, 1917*, 179–80.

79 Both documents reprinted in Alexander Shlyapnikov, *Semnadtsatyi god*, 4:259–60, 263.

80 Allen, *Alexander Shlyapnikov, 1885–1937*, 89–90; Rabinowitch, *Prelude to Revolution*, 54–79; Wade, *Russian Revolution, 1917*, 179–80.

81 Both documents reprinted in Alexander Shlyapnikov, *Semnadtsatyi god*, 4:282, 300.

82 Allen, *Alexander Shlyapnikov, 1885–1937*, 82–83; Wade, *Red Guards and Workers' Militias*, 97–99, 133–37.

83 Shlyapnikov, *Semnadtsatyi god*, 4:128–29.

84 *Semnadtsatyi god*, 4:128.

85 Alexander Shlyapnikov, "Worker Guard," *Pravda*, no. 44 (April 29, 1917): 9–10.

86 Anonymous, "About the Red Guard," *Rabochaia gazeta*, no. 43 (April 29, 1917): 1–2. In that final line, the first phrase is "Shumim, bratets, shumim!" from A. S. Griboedov's 1824 comedy *Gore ot uma* (*Woe from Wit*). The second phrase derives from "Après nous, le deluge," attributed to French King Louis XV or his mistress.

87 A. Belenin (Alexander Shlyapnikov), "About the Red Guard," *Pravda*, no. 49 (May 5, 1917): 4.

88 Published in Alexander Shlyapnikov, *Semnadtsatyi god*, 4:256.

89 Shlyapnikov, *Semnadtsatyi god*, 4:257.

90 Allen, *Alexander Shlyapnikov, 1885–1937*, 85–92.

91 Shlyapnikov uses the adjective *mestnicheskaia*, which can be used pejoratively to mean "regionalism" or "giving preference to local interests." It is the adjectival form of the noun *mestnichestvo*—a Muscovite Russian method of ranking nobles in state service according to their ancestors' and family members' rank and responsibilities.

92   He seems to be referring to methods of making the human body more machinelike.

93   Shlyapnikov, "Nash tarif," 3–6.

94   Alexander Shlyapnikov, "We Should Have Only One Union of Metalworkers," *Metallist*, nos. 1–2 (August 17, 1917): 13–14.

95   Alexander Shlyapnikov, "Tasks of the Wage Rates Valuation Commissions," *Metallist*, no. 3 (October 1, 1917): 3–4.

96   Alexander Shlyapnikov, "Once More about the Organization of Unions," *Metallist*, no. 5 (November 9, 1917): 2.

97   A paragraph about Moscow metalworkers' union membership numbers is omitted.

98   Probably Petr Smidovich, a Bolshevik, and Boris Kibrik, a Menshevik.

99   Alexander Shlyapnikov, "About the Conference of the Metalworkers' Union of Moscow Oblast," *Metallist*, no. 5 (November 9, 1917): 10–12. Remaining points on the agenda are omitted from this translation.

100 Alexander Shlyapnikov, "To All Workers," *Izvestia*, December 22, 1917, 11.

101 Rabinowitch, *Bolsheviks Come to Power*, 309–10.

102 GARF, f. 130, op. 1, d. 1, l. 20, November 28, 1917.

103 Alexander Rabinowitch, *The Bolsheviks in Power: The First Year of Soviet Rule in Petrograd* (Bloomington: Indiana University Press, 2007), 88–91; Alexander Shlyapnikov, "Pamiati 'uchredilki,'" *Ogonek* 5, no. 44 (1924): 9–10.

104 Sheila Fitzpatrick, *The Russian Revolution*, 4th ed. (Oxford: Oxford University Press, 2017), 73.

105 Rabinowitch, *Bolsheviks in Power*, 97, 106–9.

106 Rabinowitch, *Bolsheviks in Power*, 98; Jonathan D. Smele, *The "Russian" Civil Wars, 1916–1926: Ten Years That Shook the World* (Oxford: Oxford University Press, 2017), 54, 58–59; Wade, *Red Guards and Workers' Militias*, 314, 319.

107 Fitzpatrick, *The Russian Revolution*, 76-77; Wade, *Red Guards and Workers' Militias*, 331.

108 Rabinowitch, *Bolsheviks in Power*, 190–91; Wade, *Red Guards and Workers' Militias*, 329.

109 Wade, *Red Guards and Workers' Militias*, 312, 327, 330.

110 Rabinowitch, *Bolsheviks in Power*, 291–92, 296; Wade, *Red Guards and Workers' Militias*, 317.

111 Wade, *Red Guards and Workers' Militias*, 331–32.

112 GARF, f. 130, op. 1, d. 1, l. 1, November 15, 1917; f. 382, op. 1, d. 17, ll. 1–4, 34; Shlyapnikov, "K oktiabriu," 35; V. V. Obolensky (N. Osinsky), "Iz pervykh dnei VSNKh," *Narodnoe khoziaistvo*, no. 11 (1918): 11, 14; Samuel A. Oppenheim, "The Supreme Economic Council, 1917–1921," *Soviet Studies* 25, no. 1 (1973): 15.

113 VTsSPS, *Pervyi vserossiiskii syezd professionalnykh soiuzov, 7-14 ianvaria 1918; polnyi stenograficheskii otchet s predisloviem M. Tomskogo* (Moscow: VTsSPS, 1918),

3; Smith, *Red Petrograd*, 217; Edward Hallett Carr, *The Bolshevik Revolution, 1917–1923*, vol. 2 (London: Macmillan, 1952), 111.

114 RGASPI, f. 17, op. 1a, d. 119, l. 8, letter from Shlyapnikov to the CC, January 11, 1918; Iu. Gambarov et al., eds., *Deiateli SSSR i oktiabr'skoi revoliutsii: avtobiografii i biografii*, vol. 2 of 3 (Moscow: Granat, [1927–29] 1989), 230–32; Jonathan Beecher and Valerii N. Fomichev, "French Socialism in Lenin's and Stalin's Moscow: David Ryazanov and the French Archive of the Marx-Engels Institute," *Journal of Modern History* 1 (2006): 143.

115 Alexander Shlyapnikov, "Novyi tarif rabochikh-metallistov," *Metallist*, no. 2 (February 19, 1918): 14; GARF, f. 382, op. 1, d. 17, l. 4.

116 Shlyapnikov, "K oktiabriu," 33; Alexander Shlyapnikov, "V.I. Lenin i Narkomtrud (po lichnym vospominaniiam)," *Voprosy truda* 3 (1924): 4; Shkliarevsky, *Labor in the Russian Revolution*, 119, 160.

117 Shkliarevsky, *Labor in the Russian Revolution*, 119–23, 128–29, 160.

118 Smith, *Red Petrograd*, 220–23; GARF, f. 382, op. 1, d. 17, l. 3.

119 Jay Sorenson, *The Life and Death of Soviet Trade Unionism: 1917–1928* (New York: Atherton Press, 1969), 53.

120 GARF, f. 382, op. 1, d. 17, l. 3.

121 Workers paid by piece rates were paid per unit of product rather than by an hourly rate.

122 Smith, *Red Petrograd*, 132–33; Alexander Shlyapnikov, "Zadachi rastsenochnykh komissii," *Metallist*, no. 3 (October 1, 1917): 3.

123 RGASPI, f. 19, op. 1, d. 100, ll. 4, 12, 20 April 1918; Oppenheim, "The Supreme Economic Council, 1917–1921," 6–8.

124 RGASPI, f. 17, op. 4, d. 180, l. 5.

INDEX

ABOUT HAYMARKET BOOKS

Haymarket Books is a radical, independent, nonprofit book publisher based in Chicago.

Our mission is to publish books that contribute to struggles for social and economic justice. We strive to make our books a vibrant and organic part of social movements and the education and development of a critical, engaged, international left.

We take inspiration and courage from our namesakes, the Haymarket martyrs, who gave their lives fighting for a better world. Their 1886 struggle for the eight-hour day—which gave us May Day, the international workers' holiday—reminds workers around the world that ordinary people can organize and struggle for their own liberation. These struggles continue today across the globe—struggles against oppression, exploitation, poverty, and war.

Since our founding in 2001, Haymarket Books has published more than five hundred titles. Radically independent, we seek to drive a wedge into the risk-averse world of corporate book publishing. Our authors include Noam Chomsky, Arundhati Roy, Rebecca Solnit, Angela Y. Davis, Howard Zinn, Amy Goodman, Wallace Shawn, Mike Davis, Winona LaDuke, Ilan Pappé, Richard Wolff, Dave Zirin, Keeanga-Yamahtta Taylor, Nick Turse, Dahr Jamail, David Barsamian, Elizabeth Laird, Amira Hass, Mark Steel, Avi Lewis, Naomi Klein, and Neil Davidson. We are also the trade publishers of the acclaimed Historical Materialism Book Series and of Dispatch Books.

ALSO AVAILABLE FROM HAYMARKET BOOKS

1905, Leon Trotsky

Alexander Shlyapnikov, 1885–1937, Barbara C. Allen

Alexandra Kollontai: A Biography, Cathy Porter

The Bolsheviks Come to Power, Alexander Rabinowitch

Clara Zetkin: Selected Writings, Clara Zetkin, edited by Philip S. Foner, foreword by Angela Y. Davis and Rosalyn Baxandall

Eyewitnesses to the Russian Revolution, edited by Todd Chretien

History of the Russian Revolution, Leon Trotsky

Lenin's Moscow, by Alfred Rosmer, translated by Ian Birchall

Lenin's Political Thought, Neil Harding

Lessons of October, Leon Trotsky

October Song: Bolshevik Triumph, Communist Tragedy, 1917–1924, Paul Le Blanc

Red Petrograd: Revolution in the Factories, 1917–1918, S. A. Smith

Reminiscences of Lenin, Nadezhda K. Krupskaya

Revolution and Counterrevolution: Class Struggle in a Moscow Metal Factory, Kevin Murphy

Revolution in Danger, Victor Serge

Year One of the Russian Revolution, Victor Serge